Deck 8   Deck 7   Deck (

 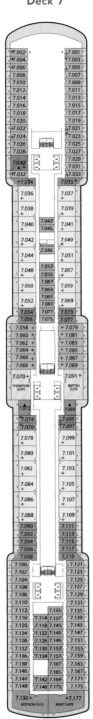 

VORN / FORWARD

MITTSCHIFFS / MIDSHIP

ACHTERN / AFT

Schiffsdaten	Technical Data
Taufe: 11. Oktober 2010	Naming Ceremony: 11th October 2010
Jungfernfahrt: 12. Oktober 2010	Maiden Voyage: 12th October 2010
Flagge: Großbritannien	Flag: Great Britain
Tonnage: 92000 BRZ	Grosstonnage: 92000 BRZ
Länge: 294 Meter	Length: 294 Meter
Breite: 32 Meter	Beam: 32 Meter
Tiefgang: 8 Meter	Draft: 8 Meter
Geschwindigkeit: max. 23,7 Knoten	Max Speed: max. 23,7 Knots
Passagierkapazität: 2068	Max Passenger: 2068
Kabinenzahl: 1034	Max Cabins: 1034
Crew-Mitglieder: 1003	Nob. of Crew: 1003

DELIUS KLASING

Ingo Thiel

QUEEN ELIZABETH

Noble Eleganz zur See
Elegance at Sea

Delius Klasing Verlag

Außerdem sind von Ingo Thiel im Delius Klasing Verlag erschienen:
Queen Victoria, Königliches Ambiente auf See
Fofftein, Reportagen und Geschichten aus dem Hamburger Hafen

Bibliografische Information der Deutschen Nationalbibliothek
Die Deutsche Nationalbibliothek verzeichnet diese Publikation
in der Deutschen Nationalbibliografie; detaillierte bibliografische
Daten sind im Internet über http://dnb.d-nb.de abrufbar.

1. Auflage
ISBN 978-3-7688-3322-6
© by Delius, Klasing & Co. KG, Bielefeld

Text: Ingo Thiel
Übersetzung ins Englische: Dipl.-Ing. Klaus Neumann
Lektorat: Birgit Radebold, Katharina Harde-Tinnefeld
Bildnachweis S.43 und 122/123: Frank Behling; alle übrigen Ingo Thiel und Cunard Line
Schutzumschlaggestaltung: Gabriele Engel
Layout: Cordula Kreft, scanlitho.teams
Lithografie: scanlitho.teams, Bielefeld
Druck: Kunst- und Werbedruck, Bad Oeynhausen
Printed in Germany 2011

Delius Klasing Verlag, Siekerwall 21, D - 33602 Bielefeld
Tel.: 0521/559-0, Fax: 0521/559-115
E-Mail: info@delius-klasing.de
www.delius-klasing.de

INHALT

CONTENT

DIE DRITTE
QUEEN ELIZABETH

THE THIRD
QUEEN ELIZABETH

Der Name *Queen Elizabeth* lässt bei Schiffsliebhabern in der ganzen Welt die Herzen höher schlagen. Zweimal bereits trugen Schiffe der Reederei Cunard Line diesen Namen, und beides waren Ozeanliner mit einer außergewöhnlich schönen Linienführung – der Inbegriff von Eleganz. Beide Liner verzeichneten Rekorde und schrieben Geschichte: Die erste *Queen Elizabeth* war bei ihrer Indienststellung 1938 mit 83 637 GT das größte Passagierschiff und hielt diesen Titel bis 1996. Sie war der Star der Atlantikroute und dominierte die Strecke von der Alten in die Neue Welt und zurück gemeinsam mit der *Queen Mary* bis zum Siegeszug der Langstreckenflieger in den 1960er-Jahren.

Die *Queen Elizabeth 2* (von ihren Fans kurz *QE 2* genannt) war der letzte echte Ozeanliner, auf dem die Träume vergangener Luxus-Schiffsreisen wahr wurden. Erinnerungen an eine Epoche, als Reisende noch Zeit mitbrachten und die Muße, das Leben an Bord zu genießen. Sie war so populär wie kein anderes Passagierschiff ihrer Zeit und hält den Fahrtrekord für Passagierschiffe: Als die legendäre alte Lady am 27. November 2008 in Dubai zum letzten Mal anlegte, hatte sie in 41 Jahren, 2 Monaten und 7 Tagen mehr als 5,6 Millionen Seemeilen mit 2,5 Millionen Passagieren zurückgelegt und 26 Weltreisen sowie 805 Atlantiküberquerungen absolviert.

Beide Queens repräsentierten auch immer ihr Land, als jeweiliges Flaggschiff der britischen Handelsflotte und im

All over the world, the name *Queen Elizabeth* makes ship lovers' hearts beat faster. Already twice, ships of the shipping company Cunard Line carried this name, and both were ocean liners with an exceptional beautiful silhouette – the embodiment of elegance. Both liners achieved a number of records and created history: on her launch in 1938, the first *Queen Elizabeth,* measured 83,637 GRT and was the largest passenger ship. She held onto this title until 1996. She was the star on the Atlantic route and dominated the route from the Old to the New World and back together with *Queen Mary* until the triumph of long-haul aircraft in the sixties.

Queen Elizabeth 2 (referred to as *QE 2* by her fans) was the last true ocean liner, through which the dreams of luxury ship voyages of yesteryears became true. This evokes fond memories of an era, when travellers still had plenty of leisure time to savour in life's magnificent moments aboard a luxury liner. She was more popular than any other passenger ship of her time and held onto the speed record for passenger ships. On 27th November 2008, after 41 years, 2 months and 7 days, when the legendary Old Lady was moored for the final time in Dubai, she had already covered a distance of more than 5.6 million nautical miles with 2.5 million passengers on board, including 26 world voyages as well as 805 Atlantic crossings.

Both Queens represented their country as respective flagships of the British merchant fleet and served as troop

Während der Jungfernsaison wurde die
Queen Elizabeth bei ihren Erstanläufen in
jedem Hafen feierlich empfangen, wie
hier in Fort Lauderdale, wo Löschboote
dem Liner zu Ehren Fontänen sprühten.

On her maiden calls *Queen Elizabeth*
was received with festivities in every
port: here in Fort Lauderdale, where
the fire-fighting boats sprayed water
jets in honour of the Queen.

Kriegseinsatz als Truppentransporter; die *Queen Elizabeth* im Zweiten Weltkrieg, die QE 2 im Falkland-Krieg. Schon bei der Taufe des ersten Schiffes 1938 war die britische Monarchin Queen Elizabeth II. zugegen, die QE 2 taufte sie 1967 ebenso selbst wie 2010 die neue *Queen Elizabeth*. Das 237. Schiff seit der Gründung der britischen Traditionsreederei Cunard im Jahre 1840 ist mit 92 000 BRZ nach der *Queen Mary 2* der zweitgrößte jemals gebaute Cunard-Liner.

Mit dem Neuzugang verfügte die älteste noch bestehende Passagierreederei mit Transatlantikroute zu diesem Zeitpunkt über die weltweit jüngste Kreuzfahrtflotte. Gemeinsam mit der *Queen Mary 2* und der *Queen Victoria* soll die dritte *Queen Elizabeth* ein neues Zeitalter der Ozeanliner starten und in einem stetig wachsenden Kreuzfahrtmarkt mit nostalgischen Werten bei gleichzeitig modernster Technik und Unterhaltung punkten. Galaabende in festlicher Garderobe,

carriers; during World War II, *QE 2* also during the Falklands War. Her Majesty Queen Elizabeth II was already present when the first ship was launched in 1938. In 1967, she launched *QE 2* and the new *Queen Elizabeth* in 2010. The company's 237th ship, ever since the traditional British shipping line had been established in 1840, measuring 92,000 RT, is the second largest Cunard liner ever built, excluding *Queen Mary 2*. Adding this newcomer to its fleet able the oldest existing passenger shipping company was able to offer on the Transatlantic route the youngest cruise fleet in the world. Together with *Queen Mary 2* and *Queen Victoria*, the third *Queen Elizabeth* will enter a new era of ocean liners: eliciting nostalgic memories reinforced with state-of-the-art technology and entertainment systems in a continuously growing cruise market. Formal soirées in formal attire, gorgeous balls, classical high

rauschende Bälle, klassischer High Tea, der hochklassige White Star Service sowie eine Inneneinrichtung der öffentlichen Räume, die an die der historischen Queens angelehnt ist und auch Originalkunstwerke und -gegenstände der *QE 2* umfasst, sollen ein internationales, weltgewandtes Publikum ansprechen. Dabei hat sich das Cunard-Management mit der *Queen Elizabeth* auch auf den Markt mit dem stärksten Passagierzuwachs der vergangenen Jahre eingestellt und mit der ersten Weltreise eines Cunardschiffes ab Hamburg in 2012 für ein Novum in der langen Reedereigeschichte gesorgt. Sowohl die *QE 2* als auch die *Queen Mary 2* haben in Deutschland eine große Fangemeinde angesprochen. Die neue *Queen Elizabeth* tritt in große Fußstapfen; die nächsten Jahrzehnte werden zeigen, ob die dritte Königin dieses Namens selbst Geschichte schreiben kann.

tea, the first-class White Star service as well as the interior furnishings of the public rooms, remind us of the historical Queens and the original works cum objects of art from the *QE 2* address an international, cosmopolitan audience. With *Queen Elizabeth*, the Cunard Management focuses on the market segment showing the strongest passenger growth during the past years. For the first time in the lengthy history of the shipping company, a Cunard ship will depart on her first world voyage from Hamburg in 2012. Both *QE 2* and *Queen Mary 2* appeal to a large fan community in Germany. The new *Queen Elizabeth* enters the market with high expectations courtesy of her predecessors, and the coming decades will prove, if the third Queen bearing this prestigious name can rewrite history all by herself.

WIE ALLES BEGANN

HOW IT ALL STARTED

DER POSTBOTE IHRER MAJESTÄT

Samuel Cunard erblickte am 21. November 1787 im kanadischen Halifax als erster von fünf Brüdern das Licht der Welt. Bereits mit 17 Jahren sammelte er mit einer Gemischtwarenhandlung geschäftliche Erfahrungen, mit 21 Jahren gründete er mit seinem Vater eine Gesellschaft, die sich auf Transporte mit Schiffen spezialisierte. Als sein Vater elf Jahre später, 1819, das Geschäft an Samuel übergab, hatte das Unternehmen 40 Schiffe und unterhielt für die englische Post den Brief- und Paketservice entlang der gesamten amerikanischen Ostküste – von Neufundland bis nach Bermuda. Damit nicht genug, wurden weitere Geschäftsfelder gesucht.

Im Januar 1825 gelang der Sprung über den Pazifik: Für die Ostindische Handelsgesellschaft übernahm Cunard den Teetransport von China nach Kanada. Auch privat »expandierte« Samuel Cunard in diesen Jahren. Nach seiner Heirat 1815 gebar seine Frau neun Kinder. Als Samuel im Jahre 1828 Witwer wurde, kümmerte er sich fortan allein um seine Nachkommen. Seinen Geschäftssinn beeinträchtigte diese zusätzliche Herausforderung indes kaum: Gemeinsam mit seinen Brüdern Henry und Joseph beteiligte sich Samuel Cunard 1833 am Dampfschiff *Royal Wilhelm*, das für den regelmäßigen Personenverkehr zwischen Quebec City und der Ostküste Kanadas gebaut worden war, aber auch für Atlantiküberquerungen eingesetzt wurde – der nächste Ozean wurde in Angriff genommen. Obwohl mit Dampfmaschinen

HER MAJESTY'S POSTMAN

Samuel Cunard was born 21st November 1787 in Halifax, Canada, as the eldest of five brothers. Already at the age of 17, he had gained his first business experience in running a general store. When he was 21, he had already established a company together with his father, specialising in sea-transport. In 1819, after his father had handed over the whole shipping business into Samuel's hands, the company already owned 40 ships and undertook mail and parcel delivery services along the American East Coast from Newfoundland to Bermuda on behalf of British Mail. In January 1825, Cunard took over the tea transport from China to Canada for the East India Company. In 1828 after thirteen years of marriage his wife Susanne passed away. From then on the widower took care of his nine children alone and ran his business.

In 1833, together with his brothers Henry and Joseph, Samuel Cunard participated in the construction of the steamship *Royal Wilhelm* which was built not only for regular passenger transportation between Quebec City and the Canadian East Coast, but also for Transatlantic voyages. The *Royal Wilhelm* spent most of her time at the sea under sail, because the boilers had to be cleaned constantly. Using the sails meant that the arrival times were still depending on the weather conditions. Cunard was looking out for something more reliable and faster, so he developed a concept based on paddle-wheel steamers.

Historische Bauzeichnung des ersten
Schiffes der Cunard Line, der *Britannia*.

A historical construction plan of
Britannia, Cunard Line's first ship.

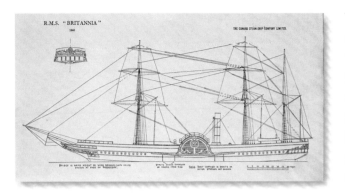

The advantage was obvious: the predictable speed permitted a regular schedule, similar to trains but at sea. In January 1839, Samuel Cunard sailed to London. On board *Reindeer* he read the newspaper »Nova Scotia« and found an invitation to tender for operating the mail service from the United Kingdom to Halifax and New York. When Cunard arrived in London, he immediately submitted his bid, although the deadline had already expired. Twelve weeks later after difficult negotiations, he won the contract, because he had additionally offered to ship the mail even during the dangerous winter season across the Atlantic. On 4th May 1839, the British Admiralty signed a contract with him for seven years. The ships had to leave on the 4th and the 19th day of each month. From November until February, one departure was guaranteed every month.

Cunard contacted Robert Napier, the owner of a shipyard which was situated on the river Clyde near Glasgow, regarding an order for three ships. However, Napier managed to convince the ship owner that an extra ship would mean more profit. Samuel Cunard found this proposal interesting. However he was not willing to bear the financial risk all alone. Therefore, Napier introduced him to two Scottish business colleagues George Burns and David McIver, who succeeded in collecting 215,000 pounds using a fund raising campaign. Cunard contributed 55,000 pounds of his own money. As a gesture of gratitude towards his investors he introduced the Scottish lion emblem into the red banner of his new fleet.

The wooden-hull ships weighed 1,156 tons with a length of 63 metres and a passenger capacity of 115. The two steam engines generated a power of 440 HP, resulting in a cruising speed of 9 knots. The orders went to different shipyards, but Napier built the engines for all four of them. On 5th February 1840, the Greenock-based Robert Duncan yard launched *Britannia*, named by Napier's niece Isabella. The *Acadia* was built by John Wood, the *Caledonia* by Charles Wood, and the *Columbia* by Robert Steele. All ships were three-mast vessels. The funnel was located between the fore and the main mast.

On 4th July 1840, *Britannia* departed on her maiden voyage from Liverpool via Halifax to Boston. There were 63 passengers on board, among them Samuel Cunard and his daughter Ann. The passage took 14 days and eight hours and was three days faster than expected. In the first year, *Britannia* and her three sister ships achieved a total of 40 Transatlantic passages, always departing on

ausgerüstet, fuhr die *Royal Wilhelm* tatsächlich meistens doch unter Segel, weil die Kessel allzu schnell verrußten und gereinigt werden mussten. Daher richteten sich die Ankunftszeiten wie bisher eher nach den Witterungsbedingungen denn nach einem festen Zeitplan. Cunard sah sich nach einer verlässlicheren und schnelleren Methode um und entwickelte ein Konzept mit Schaufelraddampfern. Der Vorteil war die vorhersagbare Geschwindigkeit, die wiederum einen regelmäßigen Fahrplan erlaubte – sozusagen eine Eisenbahn auf dem Wasser.

Im Januar 1839, Samuel Cunard segelte mit der *Reindeer* nach London, las er an Bord eine Anzeige in der Zeitung »Nova Scotia«, in welcher der Postservice zwischen dem Britischen Königreich, Halifax und New York ausgeschrieben wurde. Bedingung war eine hohe Zuverlässigkeit – und die war nur mit Dampfschiffen zu erreichen. Doch hatte Samuel nicht genau damit in Kanada gerade erst gute Erfahrungen gemacht? Kaum in London angekommen, gab Cunard sofort sein Angebot ab, obwohl die Frist bereits abgelaufen war. Nach zwölf Wochen harter Verhandlungen bekam er den Zuschlag, weil er, anders als seine Mitbewerber, freiwillig anbot, die Post auch in der gefährlichen Wintersaison auf dem Atlantik zu befördern: Am 4. Mai 1839 unterzeichnete die britische Admiralität einen Sieben-Jahres-Vertrag. Abfahrten sollten jeweils am 4. und am 19. eines Monats sein, von November bis Februar wurde immerhin eine Abfahrt pro Monat garantiert.

Eigentlich wollte Cunard drei Schiffe für diesen Deal bauen lassen und wandte sich deshalb an den Konstrukteur Robert Napier, der seine Werft auf dem Clyde bei Glasgow hatte. Napier überzeugte den Reeder jedoch schnell davon, dass mit einem Schiff mehr der Profit höher sei. Samuel Cunard war dem Vorschlag gegenüber nicht abgeneigt, scheute sich aber, das finanzielle Risiko allein zu tragen. Napier stellte ihm daraufhin zwei schottische Geschäftsmänner vor, George Burns

und David McIver, die über einen Fonds 215 000 Pfund einsammelten. Cunard legte 55 000 Pfund dazu und nahm als Dank an die Investoren den schottischen Löwen ins rote Banner der neuen Flotte.

Die Schiffe waren mit 63 Metern Länge auf 1156 Tonnen ausgelegt und sollten 115 Passagiere an Bord nehmen. Zwei Dampfmaschinen mit insgesamt 440 PS ergaben eine Betriebsgeschwindigkeit von 9 Knoten. Die Aufträge gingen an unterschiedliche Werften, Napier hatte sie aber alle gezeichnet und baute die Maschinen für alle vier. Am 5. Februar 1840 erfolgte bei Robert Duncan in Greenock der Stapellauf der *Britannia*, Taufpatin war Napiers Nichte Isabella. Die *Acadia* wurde bei John Wood gebaut, die *Caledonia* bei Charles Wood, Robert Steele legte die *Columbia* auf Kiel. Alle Schiffe waren Dreimaster, aus Holz gebaut, und bei allen dreien befand sich der Schornstein zwischen Vorder- und Hauptmast.

Die Jungfernreise der *Britannia* am 4. Juli 1840 führte von Liverpool über Halifax nach Boston. Insgesamt waren 63 Passagiere an Bord, unter ihnen Samuel Cunard mit seiner Tochter Ann. Die Passage dauerte genau 14 Tage und acht Stunden – rund drei Tage schneller als erwartet. Im ersten Jahr bewältigten die Britannia und ihre drei Schwesterschiffe zusammen 40 Atlantiküberquerungen, stets mit pünktlicher Abfahrt – eine für die damalige Zeit ebenso ungewöhnliche wie herausragende Leistung. Dass zwei dieser Schiffe zudem mit dem Blauen Band als schnellste Schiffe auf der transatlantischen Europa–New York-Route ausgezeichnet wurden, sei nur am Rande bemerkt. Nachdem 1848 ein neuer Vertrag mit der Admiralität die doppelte Postmenge und eine entsprechende Entlohnung sicherte, wurde das Hauptquartier nach London verlegt. Das erste Jahrzehnt des Bestehens schloss die Reederei mit großem Erfolg ab: 470 Atlantiküberquerungen mit mehr als 60 000 Passagieren wurden durchgeführt. Spötter nannten den Atlantik gar »Cunards Teich« – eine Bezeichnung, die dem Reeder vermutlich nicht schlecht gefiel.

1863 gab Sir Samuel nach einer Herzattacke die Geschäftsführung der Reederei an zwei seiner Söhne weiter; zuvor war er von der britischen Königin Queen Victoria aufgrund seiner Verdienste im Krimkrieg – er hatte der britischen Regierung Schiffe für den Truppentransport überlassen – zum Ritter geschlagen. Als privates Wappen wählte er nunmehr drei Anker, über denen ein Falke auf einem Felsen hockte. Am 28. April 1865 starb Samuel Cunard im Alter von 78 Jahren, seine letzte Ruhestätte befindet sich in London.

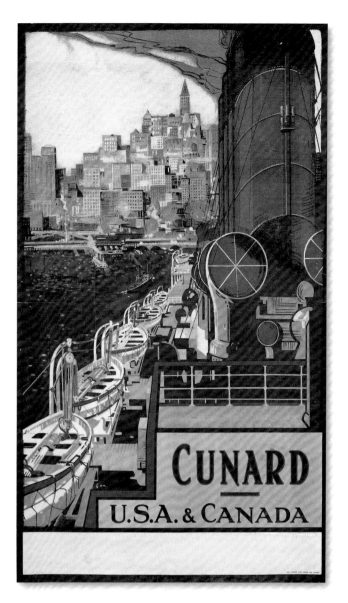

time, an unusual and outstanding novelty at that time. In 1848, Cunard's headquarters moved to London, after a new contract signed with the Admiralty secured double the volume of mail and also included an adequate compensation.

The shipping company brought the first decade of its existence to a close with immense success: 470 Transatlantic voyages with more than 60,000 passengers were carried out during its years of operation. Some mockers named the Atlantic »Cunard's pool«.

On 9th March 1859, Samuel Cunard was given a knighthood by Queen Victoria, for his meritorious deeds during the Crimean War, when he handed over some of his ships to function as military troop carriers for the British government. As his coat-of-arms he had chosen three anchors with a falcon sitting on a rock above the anchors. Sir Samuel handed over the management of the shipping company to two of his sons in 1863 after a heart attack. On 28th of April, he died at the age of 78 years and was buried in London.

Cunard Line ist stolz darauf, dass seit der Gründung 1840 alle Schiffe das offizielle Kürzel RMS (Royal Mail Ship) tragen dürfen.

From 1840 onwards, Cunard Line is proud that all its ships are allowed to use the official abbreviation R.M.S. (Royal Mail Ship).

DAS WAPPEN DER CUNARD LINE

THE EMBLEM OF THE CUNARD LINE

Das heutige Wappen der Reederei geht auf das Jahr 1879 zurück – zu diesem Zeitpunkt wurde die Cunard Line zu einer Aktiengesellschaft: der Cunard Steamship Company. Gegenüber dem Gründungswappen wurden einige Elemente hinzugefügt: Der schottische Löwe erhielt einen Globus zwischen die Pranken, der die westliche Hemisphäre mit dem Atlantik zeigt und die Routen symbolisieren sollte, welche die Cunard-Liner damals im regelmäßigen Liniendienst zwischen Alter und Neuer Welt fuhren. Neu war auch die große Krone, welche das Wappen am oberen Rand begrenzte. Das königliche Symbol steht für den Staatsdienst von Cunard Line, denn die Schiffe fahren seit der Gründung mit dem Gewinn der Ausschreibung des Postliniendienstes im Auftrag des britischen Staates, der zu dieser Zeit noch eine echte Monarchie war.

Noch heute ist die offizielle Bezeichnung der Schiffe z. B. RMS *Queen Elizabeth,* wobei RMS für Royal Mail Ship (Königliches Postschiff) steht.

Schließlich wurde beim neuen Wappen noch der Kopf des Löwen in Richtung des Betrachters gedreht, sodass er einen anschaut. Die ursprüngliche Variante des Löwen war identisch mit der des Königshauses – für eine öffentliche Gesellschaft undenkbar. Wegen dieses Löwen und seiner großen Verdienste und Geschäftserfolge wurde Samuel Cunard auch »Dampf-Löwe« (englisch Steam Lion) genannt. Bis heute fahren die Schiffe der Cunard Line unter britischer Flagge und mit diesem Wappen. Das jeweilige Flaggschiff, momentan die *Queen Mary 2,* ist übrigens gleichzeitig das Flaggschiff der britischen Handelsflotte.

The present emblem of the shipping company dates back to the year 1879 when the Cunard Line became a public company – called the Cunard Steamship Company. Deviating from the foundation emblem, some elements were added: the Scottish lion received a globe between his paws, depicting the Western Hemisphere with the Atlantic and symbolising the routes of the Cunard liners at that time in regular passenger service between the Old and the New World. The big crown, which bordered the emblem at the upper edge, was also novel. The royal symbol stands for Cunard Line's service on behalf of the state, because the ships undertook the scheduled mail service right from the origination, after the company won the bid from the British state, which at that time was still a true monarchy,

Even today, the official name of the ships shows this, i.e. RMS *Queen Elizabeth* for Royal Mail Ship. Finally, the head of the lion on the new emblem was turned towards the spectator, so that the lion faced him. The original layout was identical to that of the British Royal Family – deemed inappropriate for a public society. Because of this lion and its great efforts and associated business successes, Samuel Cunard was also called the »Steam Lion«. Even today, the ships of the Cunard Line under British flags sail with this emblem. The present flagship of the Cunard Line, currently the *Queen Mary 2,* is also simultaneously the flagship of the British merchant fleet.

Shuffleboard gehört seit den Anfängen der modernen Kreuzfahrt zu den beliebtesten Freizeitbeschäftigungen an Bord.

From the beginning of modern cruise shipping, shuffleboard is one of the most popular leisure activities on board.

Einer der Höhepunkte auf den Weltreisen war die Durchquerung des Panamakanals.

Due to very efficient stabilisers, most sports are possible on board the new *Queen Elizabeth*.

DAS QUEENS-KONZEPT

Nachdem Cunard Line den Transatlantikdienst einige Jahre lang mit der *Mauretania, Aquitania* und *Berengaria* versah, beschloss man schon Mitte der 1920er-Jahre, zukünftig nur noch zwei statt drei Schiffe wöchentlich über den Atlantik zu schicken. Da die Auslastung nach wie vor sehr gut war, mussten die beiden neuen Superliner deutlich größer sein als ihre Vorgängerinnen – und zudem schneller, denn 1928 wurde der *Mauretania* von der Bremen des Norddeutschen Lloyd das Blaue Band abgenommen. In nur fünf Tagen sollten die neuen Liner den Atlantik überqueren, dann binnen zwei Tagen Treibstoff, Wäsche und Lebensmittel bunkern und sofort auf die Rückreise gehen.

Der erste der beiden Liner, die *Queen Mary,* wurde im Dezember 1930 auf der schottischen Werft John Browne am Clyde auf Kiel gelegt. Die geplanten Kosten für die Baunummer 534 beliefen sich auf 5 Millionen Pfund, was heute etwa 300 Millionen Euro entsprechen würde. Der Bau verzögerte sich durch die Auswirkungen der Weltwirtschaftskrise, erst ein Kredit der britischen Regierung, der die Verschmelzung von Cunard Line mit der schwächelnden White Star Line zur Bedingung hatte, sorgte dafür, dass die Arbeiten auf der Werft im Sommer 1934 weitergingen. Taufpatin war am 26. September 1934 Queen Mary, Gattin von König Georg V. Zum ersten Mal wurde hier die Taufe von einem Mitglied des britischen Königshauses vorgenommen.

Auf die Tickets der Jungfernfahrt war ein regelrechter Run ausgebrochen: Es gab 2000 Plätze, doch mindestens 20 000 hätten verkauft werden können. Doch erst zwei Jahre später, am 27. Mai 1936, verließ die *Queen Mary,* damals das größte Passagierschiff der Welt, Southampton, verabschiedet von hunderttausend Zuschauern. Weil im gesamten ersten Dienstjahr ein solcher Ansturm auf das Schiff herrschte, dass es für jede Fahrt ellenlange Wartelisten gab, beschloss Cunard Line schnell, auch das geplante zweite Schiff zu bauen.

THE QUEENS' CONCEPT

The Cunard Line decided on a new concept of using only two instead of three ships for its weekly Atlantic service in the mid 1920ies. Two new superliners were meant to take over the scheduled service from the outdated *Mauritania, Aquitania* and *Berengaria,* and for this reason had to be larger and faster than their predecessors. They had to cross the Atlantic in five days and then take fuel, provisions and linen on board within two days, before departing on time on a new voyage.

The keel laying of the first of the two liners, *Queen Mary,* was in December 1930 at the Scottish shipyard John Browne on river Clyde. The planned costs for the hull number 534 were an estimated 5 million pounds, today an equivalent of approximately 300 million Euros. The construction was delayed by the impacts of the world economic crisis, and when a loan by the British government after agreeing to the condition of merger of the Cunard Line and the flagging White Star Line was approved finally, the construction works on the shipyard were resumed in the summer of 1934. Queen Mary herself, spouse of King George V, launched the ship on 26th September, 1934. It was the first time that a member of the British Royal Family launched a ship.

There was a mad rush for the tickets to participate in her maiden voyage: only 2,000 places were available, but 20,000 could have been easily sold. On 27th May 1936, *Queen Mary* left Southampton bidding farewell to hundreds of thousands of spectators. Because there was such huge demand during her entire first year of service and extremely long waiting lists for every voyage, Cunard Line decided to go ahead with building the second ship.

KAPITÄN CHRISTOPHER WELLS
CAPTAIN CHRISTOPHER WELLS

Drei zentrale Aufgaben nennt der 1956 geborene Christopher Wells, wenn man ihn nach seinem Berufsalltag fragt: zum einen natürlich die *Queen Elizabeth* sicher über die Weltmeere zu steuern, dann als oberster Gastgeber an Bord gleichzeitig auch als Public Relations Manager der britischen Traditionsreederei zu fungieren und vor allem die Mannschaft zu führen. Denn ohne die perfekt eingespielte Crew, so Wells, wäre die *Queen Elizabeth* einfach nur ein Schiff, erst durch die Besatzung wird sie zu einer Cunard-Königin.

Geboren wurde Christopher Wells in Bournemouth, aufgewachsen ist er in Poole in Dorset. Seine erste Begegnung mit einem Cunardliner hatte er bereits als Fünfjähriger, sein Vater nahm ihn auf eine Tour nach Southampton mit, wo gerade die *Queen Mary* am Kai lag. Der Knirps war beeindruckt von der Größe – mehr aber auch nicht. Seine Liebe zum Meer entwickelte er später beim Segeln, und so begann Wells gleich nach der Schule die vierjährige Kadettenausbildung an der Warsash School in Southampton, schloss diese 1978 als Zweiter Offizier ab und fuhr für Shell auf großen Gastankern. Das Kapitänspatent erhielt er 1985, außerdem ist Wells bei der britischen Marine Reserveoffizier im Rang eines Lieutenant Commander. 1992 wechselte er zur Cunard Line, fing an als Zweiter Offizier auf der *Queen Elizabeth 2* an und durchlief alle Offiziersränge bis hin zum Stabskapitän. Auf der *QE 2* traf er auch seine große Liebe, seine deutsche Frau Hedda, die ebenfalls auf der schwimmenden Legende arbeitete. Heute bereichern die drei Kinder Henry, Emily und William das englisch-deutsche Eheglück im eigenen Haus in Barnham, Sussex. Vier Monate leistet Wells Dienst auf See, danach hat der Kapitän zwei Monate frei.

Im April 2002 ging Wells für anderthalb Jahre an Land und kümmerte sich im französischen St. Nazaire um den Bau der *Queen Mary 2*. Bei der Indienststellung 2004 übernahm Wells den Posten des Stabskapitäns, am 1. April 2008 wurde er zum Kapitän der *Queen Mary 2* ernannt. Auf der Königin der Meere hat ihn am meisten stolz gemacht, »dass Menschen aus 55 Nationen friedlich zusammengearbeitet und gelebt haben – wie eine Art Miniatur-UN.« 50 Prozent seiner täglichen Arbeitszeit, so schätzt der drahtige Brite, ist Papierkram, 30 Prozent gehen für soziale Verpflichtungen drauf. So werden nicht nur ausgewählte Passagiere zum Essen an den Kapitänstisch oder zum Cocktail eingeladen, sondern Wells gratuliert auch mit persönlichen Schreiben zu Geburts- und Hochzeitstagen und muss beim Kapitänsempfang bis zu 800 Hände schütteln und für ähnlich viele Fotos bereitstehen. Die tägliche Kapitänsansage um 12.00 Uhr Schiffszeit mit Informationen zu Route, Wetter, zurückgelegter Strecke und eventuellen Sehenswürdigkeiten ist fester Bestandteil seines Tagesablaufs, selbst wenn er wegen Schlechtwetter die ganze Nacht auf der Brücke verbracht hat. Nur noch 20 Prozent seines Arbeitstages beschäftigt Wells sich mit nautischen Dingen, neben Besprechungen mit seinem Offiziersstab sind dies vor allem das Festlegen der Fahrtroute und die Überprüfung von Kartenberechnungen sowie Wetterlagen. Dazu kommen noch zahlreiche Trainingsstunden für Offiziere und Crew wie Seenotrettungs- und Feuerbekämpfungsübungen, medizinische Notfälle, Unfälle und Manöver, die der Kapitän persönlich leitet oder überprüft.

Und jeden Sonntag zelebriert er den Gottesdienst, sein Lieblingskirchenlied ist »Nun danket alle Gott«, denn das wurde auch auf seiner Hochzeit in Husum gespielt. Die nordfriesische Kleinstadt, aus der seine Frau stammt, hat es ihm angetan. Wenn er privat auf Reisen geht, dann nicht in eine der großen Weltmetropolen oder einem anderen der Traumziele der Welt, von denen er viele berufsbedingt schon gesehen hat – nein, es zieht ihn in die norddeutsche Tiefebene zu den Schwiegereltern.

Christopher Wells, born in 1956, always mentions three essential tasks when somebody questions him about his daily job routine: his first task is to steer *Queen Elizabeth* safely across the oceans, then to act as the senior host and public relations manager for the traditional British shipping company on board, and most important of all to head the crew. »Because without a perfectly coordinat-

ed crew«, says Wells, »the Queen Elizabeth will only be a ship. But only the crew will make her a Cunard-Queen«.

Christopher Wells was born in Bournemouth and grew up in Poole/Dorset. He had his first contact with a Cunard liner when he was five. His father took him out on a tour of Southampton, just when *Queen Mary* was berthed alongside the quay. The little boy was more or less impressed with her size. His love of the sea became stronger when he began sailing soon afterwards. And, when Wells had finished school, he immediately began a four-year cadet training at the Warsash School in Southampton, finishing as second officer in 1978. Then he worked on board large gas carriers for Shell. He received his Master's certificate in 1985. Wells is also a Reserve Officer of the Royal Navy, his rank: Lieutenant Commander. In 1992, he started working for Cunard Line. He began as second officer on board *Queen Elizabeth 2* and progressed through all the officer's ranks up to staff captain. On board *QE 2*, he also found his true love, his German wife Hedda, who worked on board the floating legend too. Today, the English-German couple enjoy marital with their own home in Barnham, Sussex, together with their three children Henry, Emily and William. Captain Wells serves on board for four months, followed by a vacation of two months.

In April 2002, Wells spent one and a half years ashore in order to supervise the construction of *Queen Mary 2* in St. Nazaire/France. On her commissioning in 2004, Wells became staff captain, and on 1st April 2008 he was appointed Captain of *Queen Mary 2*. He is very proud that people from 55 nations on board this »*Queen of the Seas*« work and live peacefully together – like a kind of a mini United Nations.

The wiry Brit estimates that 50 percent of his daily working time is just paperwork and another 30 percent is needed for performing his social duties. Not only are special passengers invited to dine at the captain's table or join him for a cocktail, Wells has to send a personal card when passengers have a birthday or wedding anniversary. During the captain's reception he has to shake up to 800 hands and be available for the same number of photo sessions. The daily captain's announcement at 12.00 h (ship's time), providing information about the route, weather, covered distance and possible places of interest, forms an integral part

of his daily routine, even if he has spent the previous night entirely on the bridge because of bad weather. Only the remaining 20 percent of his daily job hours are occupied by nautical matters: discussions with his officers, the routing, review of chart calculations and the weather forecast. Furthermore, the captain supervises numerous training sessions for the officers and crew i.e. emergency and fire fighting drills, actions in the event of medical emergencies, accidents and manoeuvres. Every Sunday, he enjoys being in charge of the church service. And his favourite song »Now thank we all our God« is played every time. This song was also played at his church wedding in Husum. He is really impressed with the small North-Frisian town, where his wife comes from. His private travel destinations do not include big cities or exotic locations – typical dream holiday spots, which he has already seen during his official voyages. No, he much rather enjoys staying at his parents-in-law's home in Northern Germany.

KÖNIGLICHE HOHEITEN

THE ROYAL FAMILY

DIE SCHÖNE: *QUEEN ELIZABETH*

Der neue Liner sollte *Queen Elizabeth* heißen, der Auftrag für den Bau ging erneut an John Brown. Die Baunummer 552 wurde mit 301 Metern nur etwas kürzer als die *Queen Mary* (310 m), während Breite (36,14 m) und Tiefgang (13 m) gleich blieben. Die Unterschiede zwischen beiden Schiffen waren von außen deutlich zu erkennen: Der Bug der *Queen Elizabeth* war schärfer geschnitten, sie hatte viel weniger Belüftungsschächte auf den Decks und nur zwei statt drei Schornsteine wie die *Queen Mary*. Mit 83 673 Tonnen war sie das größte Passagierschiff der Welt. Bis zu 2283 Passagiere und eine Crew von 1100 Mann konnte sie tragen. Die Kiellegung erfolgte am 6. Oktober 1932, an der Taufe rund sechs Jahre später, am 27. September 1938, nahm König Georg VI. teil, dessen Frau Königin Elizabeth Taufpatin war. Die endgültige Fertigstellung des Liners mitsamt der prunkvollen Innenausbauten geriet jedoch ins Stocken: Die Werftarbeiter wurden für andere Aufgaben gebraucht, denn es drohte Krieg, und die Kriegsschiffe der britischen Marine sollten schnellstmöglich überholt werden. Endgültig wurden die Arbeiten an der *Queen Elizabeth* eingestellt, nachdem Hitler am 1. September 1939 seine Truppen in Polen einmarschieren ließ – der Zweite Weltkrieg hatte begonnen.

Was dann folgte, war in der Geschichte von Luxuslinern einmalig. Nachdem zunächst nicht klar war, was mit dem erst halbfertigen Schiff geschehen sollte, verfügte der damalige Marineminister Winston Churchill, den Bau zu vollenden und das Schiff als Truppentransporter zu nutzen. Von da an war absolute Geheimhaltung oberste Priorität. Zur Täuschung der deutschen Luftwaffe wurde das Gerücht ge-

THE BEAUTY: *QUEEN ELIZABETH*

The new liner will be named *Queen Elizabeth* and the order went to John Brown once again. The hull number 552, 301 metres in length, was built slightly shorter than *Queen Mary* (310 m), while the beam (36.14 m) and the draft (13 m) remained unchanged. The differences between both ships could be clearly recognized from the outside: the bow of *Queen Elizabeth* was sharper cut. There were significantly lesser ventilation flues on the decks and she only had two instead of three funnels on *Queen Mary*. She was the world's largest passenger ship with a displacement of 83,673 tons, room for up to 2,283 passengers and a crew of 1,100. The keel laying was on 6th October 1932, followed by the launch ceremony on 27th September 1938 in the presence of King George VI and his spouse Queen Elizabeth, who named the ship. However, the final completion of the liner including all interior fittings could not be finished on time as planned earlier. The workers at the shipyard were needed for other jobs, because the warships of the Royal Navy had to be overhauled as soon as possible, as war was pending. The construction works for *Queen Elizabeth* were stopped soon after Hitler's troops invaded Poland on 1st September 1939. The Second World War had begun.

There was a dispute in the English parliament about the intended use of the half-finished *Queen Elizabeth* steam, when Churchill, the Minister of Naval Affairs at that time, decided to complete the ship so that she could be used as a troop carrier. Due to secrecy trial runs were cancelled, so the maiden voyage was to be the only available trial run. As the news of ship's completion could not be kept secret from the

Wegen ihres langen und schärferen Bugs sah die *Queen Elizabeth* viel schnittiger aus als ihre ältere und etwas kürzere Schwester (oben).

Because of her long and leaner bow *Queen Elizabeth* looked more rakish than her older and shorter sister (top).

Mit dem Stapellauf der *Queen Elizabeth* am 27. September 1938 begann für die Reederei die erfolgreiche Ära der neuen Superliner (unten).

The launch of *Queen Elizabeth* on 27th September 1938 marked the beginning of the success-ful era of the company's new super liners (bottom).

Während des Krieges konnten bis zu
12 000 Soldaten pro Fahrt aufgenommen werden – eine gewaltige
logistische Herausforderung.

Up to 12,000 soldiers could be carried
on every voyage – an enormous logisti-
cal challenge.

streut, das Schiff werde zu einem bestimmten Termin nach Southampton gebracht, um dort vollendet zu werden. Um die Scharade perfekt zu machen, wurden sogar Container mit Möbeln und Betten angeliefert sowie Unterkünfte und Verpflegung für Hunderte von schnell zusammengezogenen Arbeitern bereitgestellt. Tatsächlich verlief alles nach Plan: Um den angeblichen Ankunftstermin tauchten deutsche Bomber über Southampton auf, bis sie realisierten, dass das Schiff nicht kommen würde – es war stattdessen am 2. März 1940 bei unsichtigem Wetter und mit vier Zerstörern als Geleitschutz direkt vom Firth of Clyde aufgebrochen – die Probefahrt der *Queen Elizabeth* war zeitgleich ihre Jungfernfahrt. Nach 200 Meilen absoluter Funkstille und obligatorischem Zickzackkurs drehten die Zerstörer ab und ließen die neue Queen den Rest des Atlantiks allein bewältigen. Die Geheimhaltung war so perfekt, dass fünf Tage später ein Aufklärungsflugzeug der Trans World Airlines ziemlich überrascht war, 40 Seemeilen vor der US-Küste ein riesiges graues Schiff auszumachen. Die Nachricht verbreitete sich wie ein Lauffeuer. Tausende Zuschauer hatten sich am Hafen versammelt, als die »Queen Incognito«, wie die »New York Times« das Schiff taufte, am Pier 90 anlegte.

Anschließend fuhr der Liner weiter nach San Francisco, wo aufwendige Umbaumaßnahmen getroffen wurden: Statt luxuriösem Interieur wurden mehrstöckige Feldbetten festgeschweißt. Kabinen, die ursprünglich für bequem reisende Paare gedacht waren, wurden nunmehr Herberge für 21 Männer. Als die *Queen Elizabeth* San Francisco verließ, konnte sie bis zu 12 000 Soldaten aufnehmen – das ur-

Germans and their secret agents, a rumour was spread that *Queen Elizabeth* would be transferred to Southampton for further interior furnishing works. For this reason, containers with beds and other furniture were delivered to the shipyard. Hundreds of workers were grouped together arrangements were made for their accommodation and food supplies. The plan was successful. The German air force's bombers appeared above Southampton on the prescheduled voyage date and for the next three days in succession, before they realised, that the ship was not going to come. *Queen Elizabeth* departed Firth of Clyde in bad weather on 2nd March 1940, escorted by four destroyers and dozens of aircraft. 200 miles further west, the convoy escort left the ship, and from thereon the *Queen Elizabeth* was all alone on her way to New York. Radio Silence and a mandatory zigzag course were strictly adhered to. It was a big surprise, when on 7th May a Trans World Airlines' DC 3 discovered a huge grey ship 40 miles off the US coast. The message spread like wildfire and thousands of spectators came to witness the »Queen Incognito«, the name New York Times called her, as she was moored alongside pier 90.

Queen Elizabeth was fitted out in San Francisco to be able to accommodate up to 12,000 soldiers – more than a whole division. Welded metal frames with fold-up berths made of cloth were installed on board the liner, and a former double cabin was now able to accommodate 21 men. It needed a lot of planning. And in addition to the berths, washing facilities, toilets and laundries were also installed. During World War II, *Queen Elizabeth* covered a distance of more than 500,000 nautical miles and carried more than 700,000 men.

After the war, the Queen first carried the troops back home, that had been fighting in Europe. Later, a new clientèle came on board following the troops: English women, who had fallen in love with American and Canadian soldiers during the war and their children. On these »bride and baby voyages«, approximately 50,000 soldiers' brides and their children were shipped to their new homes in the USA and in Canada. In September 1946, her military mission was finished. On 16th October 1946, *Queen Elizabeth* left on her maiden voyage as a passenger ship, with guests on board. Some of these had bought tickets for the maiden voyage years ago, but these had been cancelled due to the war.

For the time being, aircraft on the Atlantic route had posed no real threat. However, this changed abruptly after the entry

sprüngliche Konzept, das erst Jahre später verwirklicht werden konnte, sah lediglich 2283 Passagiere vor. Nachdem sie während des Zweiten Weltkriegs mehr als 700 000 Mann befördert hatte – aufgrund ihrer hohen Geschwindigkeit war sie vor den deutschen U-Booten sicher und konnte ohne Geleitschutz fahren – und dabei rund 500 000 Seemeilen zurückgelegt hatte, versah sie anschließend auch noch Dienst als »Braut- und Babytransport«, was nichts anderes bedeutete, als die englischen Frauen und ihre zumeist noch sehr kleinen Kinder und Babys zum Zwecke der Familienzusammenführung zu ihren im Krieg kennengelernten Männern der US-amerikanischen und kanadischen Truppen zu bringen. Unter der Leitung des Roten Kreuzes reisten so rund 50 000 Soldatenfrauen und -kinder in ihre neue Heimat auf der anderen Seite des Atlantiks. Mit einem Luxusliner hatte die Queen Elizabeth in ihren ersten Dienstjahren also herzlich wenig zu tun.

Ihre tatsächliche Jungfernreise als Ozeanliner unternahm die Queen Elizabeth erst im Oktober 1946 – einen Monat nach Beendigung ihres Kriegseinsatzes. Statt Soldaten oder Kriegsbräuten kam nun endlich die Art Passagiere an Bord, für die das Schiff ursprünglich konzipiert worden war. Einige von ihnen hatten ihr Ticket bereits acht Jahre zuvor erworben …

Rund 20 Jahre lang versah die Queen Elizabeth ihren Dienst als Transatlantikliner, in denen sie mehr als 3,5 Millionen Seemeilen im Kielwasser gelassen, 2,3 Millionen Passagiere befördert und 879 Atlantiküberquerungen in Friedenszeiten absolviert hatte. Dann jedoch sah sich Cunard aufgrund der inzwischen ernstzunehmenden Konkurrenz durch Langstreckenlinienflüge gezwungen, auf neue Konzepte – und neuere Schiffe – zurückzugreifen.

Im November 1968 wurde die Queen Elizabeth aus dem Dienst der Reederei entlassen und wechselte in den Besitz von C.Y. Tung, einem Geschäftsmann aus Hongkong. Dieser wollte den schönen Liner zu einer Hochschule für Meereskunde nebst Ausbildungsstätte für Marinekadetten umbauen. Das Schiff lag bereits in Hongkong vor Anker, als es jedoch komplett ausbrannte. Spätere Ermittlungen legten den Verdacht auf Brandstiftung nahe. Als aufgrund der extremen Hitze gar die stählerne Struktur des Riesen zu schmelzen begann, brach alles in sich zusammen, und das Schiff sank mit 45° Schlagseite auf Grund. Mehr als zwei Jahre benötigte eine japanische Firma für die Abwrackarbeiten.

of long-haul aircraft into the market. In 1965, approximately four million people flew across the Atlantic, while only 650,000 travelled by ship. One year earlier, Cunard Line had signed a contract for building a new ship: for this reason, Queen Elizabeth was sold off in November 1968. That ended her 30-year career having sailed more than 3.5 million nautical miles with 2.3 million passengers on board and 879 Atlantic crossings in peaceful times. Firstly, businessmen in Florida had intended to use the liner as a hotel ship, however that project failed. Finally, Queen Elizabeth was sold off to C.Y. Tung, a Hong Kong-based businessman, in 1970. Tung had the vision to establish a university of Marine Sciences and also a Training Centre for navy cadets, with the name »Seawise University«. The ship was made seaworthy again and transferred to Hong Kong via Aruba, Rio de Janeiro and Cape Town. Queen Elizabeth took her final mooring in Hong Kong. There she would have been reconstructed, but on 9th January 1972 several fires broke out on her. Later investigations suspected arson, as the fire had broken out at five different places almost simultaneously. Within one hour, the entire ship was ablaze, and it was impossible to extinguish the fire during the night and also the day after. The steel girders and frames had melted away, the ship had collapsed and had sunk to the bottom of the harbour, where it was lying burnt out at an angle of 45 degrees. A Japanese scrap company required more than two years to totally clear away the wreck.

MOTOREN UND ANTRIEB
ENGINES AND PROPULSION

Die Energiegewinnung erfolgt durch Motoren des zum amerikanischen Caterpillar-Konzern gehörenden deutschen Schiffsmotorenherstellers Maschinenbau aus Kiel (MaK). Vier Motoren des Typs MaK 12M43C und zwei MaK 8M43C Viertakt-Diesel-Motoren treiben mit zusammen insgesamt 64 000 kW einen elektrischen Generator an, der auf Deck D, dem untersten Deck des Schiffes, untergebracht ist. Die 12M43C sind V12-zylindrig, während die 8M43C acht Zylinder besitzen. Die V12-Motoren produzieren 12 000 kW, die Achtzylinder 8000 kW. Jede dieser Maschinen hat eine 430 Millimeter Bohrung und einen Hub von 610 Millimeter bei 514 Umdrehungen pro Minute. Auf See werden die Motoren mit Schweröl betrieben. Die größeren Maschinen verbrennen 2,17 Tonnen pro Stunde, während die kleineren 1,63 Tonnen je Stunde verbrauchen. Bevor das Schweröl in den Motor eintritt, wird es gefiltert, um feste Partikel und mögliche Wasserreste zu entfernen. Danach wird es auf 125 °C erhitzt, um die Viskosität zu reduzieren und die komplette Verbrennung zu garantieren. Durch eine variable Nockenwellensteuerung der Motoren wird sichergestellt, dass in allen Lastbereichen kein sichtbarer Rauch ausgestoßen wird und die Stickoxid-Emissionen unter den Grenzwerten der International Maritime Organization (IMO) liegen. Die Motoren dieser Baureihe können zudem bei Bedarf jederzeit auf den Low Emission Engine-Standard für schadstoffarme Motoren umgerüstet werden. Liegt das Schiff im Hafen, wird auf Dieselverbrauch umgeschaltet. Dann läuft lediglich eine Maschine, um den Betrieb von Küchen, Wäscherei, Lagern, Beleuchtung, Klimaanlage, Elektrizität in den Kabinen sowie weiterer Verbrauchsstellen zu gewährleisten. Die Queen Elizabeth kann bis zu 3456 Kubikmeter Schweröl lagern, was ihr ermöglicht, 17 Tage ohne Zwischenstopp auf dem Meer zu verbringen. Die Motoren speisen Generatoren, welche die Energie in Strom umwandeln, insgesamt 63,4 Megawatt. Davon werden 11 Megawatt für den Hotelbetrieb genutzt, 48 Megawatt für den Antrieb, der Rest steht als Reserve zur Verfügung. Alle Generatoren sind mit dem Hauptschaltpult verbunden, von wo die Hauptantriebstransformatoren sowie die gesamte Elektrik des Schiffes bedient werden. Wie viele von ihnen angeschaltet werden, hängt von der von der Brücke vorgegebenen Geschwindigkeit und der vorhandenen Elektrizität ab.

Der Antrieb erfolgt über zwei Azipods Z 8040, die von ABB in Finnland gebaut wurden. Ein Azipod (Azimuthing Electric Propulsion Drive, kurz Pods, auf Deutsch etwa mit drehbarer elektrischer Vortrieb zu übersetzen) ist ein ausgelagertes Antriebssystem. Es beinhaltet einen elektrischen Motor, der an einer extrem kurzen Achse befestigt ist und eine feste Schraube antreibt. Das Konzept der Kombination von Antrieb und Lenkung erhöht die Manövrierfähigkeit und Ökonomie. Jeder Pod ist von vier hydraulisch angetriebenen Motoren gesteuert. Die beiden Gondeln sind um 360 Grad drehbar, sodass die Queen Elizabeth über eine hohe Manövrierfähigkeit verfügt. Insgesamt können sie eine Maximalkraft von 17,6 Megawatt leisten. Jeder Pod wiegt 135 Tonnen und ist so groß wie ein Londoner Doppeldeckerbus. Die Antriebseinheiten sind sogar begehbar; wenn die Queen Elizabeth im Hafen liegt, klettern regelmäßig Mechaniker und Elektriker zu Routinekontrollen hinein.

Zusammen mit den drei Bugstrahlrudern, die bei bis zu 300 Umdrehungen pro Minute je bis zu 2,2 Megawatt Leistung abrufen können, kann das Schiff ohne Ruderanlage, nur durch die Richtungs- und Geschwindigkeitseinstellung der Pods und Bugstrahlruder, gesteuert werden. Die Schrauben sind vor die Azipods montiert, was dafür sorgt, dass sie in »ruhiges« Wasser greifen, was einen maximalen Vortrieb ermöglicht. Jede Schraube hat einen Durchmesser von 5,5 Metern und vier miteinander verschraubte, feste Blätter aus einer Nickel-Aluminium-Bronze-Legierung. Jedes Schraubenblatt wiegt 4800 kg und wird von acht Bolzen gehalten. Die Höchstgeschwindigkeit der Queen Elizabeth liegt bei 24,3 Knoten, die Betriebsgeschwindigkeit beträgt zwischen 18 bis 21,7 Knoten. Bei Höchstgeschwindigkeit werden pro Stunde etwa 9800 Liter Schweröl verbrannt. Um das Schiff bei 21 Knoten Fahrt zum Stillstand zu bringen, werden circa sechseinhalb Minuten benötigt, das entspricht einer Strecke von 1,85 Kilometer. Ein Paar Stabilisatoren Fincantieri Riva Trigoso, je einer auf jeder Seite mit rund 20 Quadratmeter Finne, vermindern bei unruhiger See die Schiffsbewegungen. Zwei Anker sorgen für die nötige Stabilität, wenn das Schiff auf Reede liegt, zusätzlich ist ein Ersatzanker an Bord.

Power is generated by engines supplied by the German ship engine manufacturer Maschinenbau Kiel (MaK), a branch of the American Caterpillar group. Four engines of the type MaK 12M43C and two MaK 8M43C four stroke diesel engines producing a power of 64,000 kW drive an electric generator, which is located on deck D, the lowest deck on the ship. The 12M43C is a V12-cylinder engine, while the 8M43C features eight cylinders. The V12 engines produce 12,000 kW while the 8-cylinder generates 8,000 kW. Each of these engines has a 430 millimetres bore and a stroke of 610 millimetres at 514 rotations per minute. At sea, the engines use heavy oil. The larger engines have a fuel consumption of 2.17 tons per hour, while the smaller ones use 1.63 tons per hour. The heavy oil will be filtered to remove solid particles and residual water before it reaches the engine. After that, it is heated up to 125 degrees, in order to reduce the viscosity and to ensure complete combustion. A variable cam control of the engines avoids discharge of visible smoke at all load ranges, keeping the nitrogen oxide emissions below the critical values specified by the International Maritime Organization (IMO). If necessary, the engines of these series can be converted at any time to satisfy the low emission engine standard for low-emission engines. When the ship is moored in harbour, the power supply is switched to diesel operation. Only one engine is running then, in order to ensure the smooth operation of galleys, laundry, storage rooms, lighting, air conditioning system, power supply in the cabins and other points of consumption. *Queen Elizabeth* can bunker up to 3,456 cubic metres of heavy oil, which allows for a 17 day sea voyage without refuelling. The engines transmit their power to the generators, which transform the energy creating electric power, at a total of 63.4 megawatts. This capacity is distributed as follows: 11 megawatts for running the hotel, 48 megawatts for the propulsion, while the remaining capacity is available as reserve power. All generators are connected to the main control panel, from where the main engine transformers as well as the entire electric system of the ship can be controlled. The target speed and the available power determine how many generators need to be switched on.

The propulsion system consists of two Z 8040 azipods, built by ABB in Finland. An azipod (Azimuthing Electric Propulsion Drive, in short pod) propulsion system is outside the ship's hull. It includes an electric engine, which is attached to an extremely short shaft and is driven by a fixed propeller. The concept of the combination of propulsion and steering increases the manoeuvrability and economy. Each pod is controlled by four hydraulically driven engines. Both pods of *Queen Elizabeth* can be rotated 360 degrees, providing a high manoeuvrability and a maximum power of 17.6 megawatts. Each pod weighs 135 tons and is as large as a London Double-Decker bus. When *Queen Elizabeth* is moored in harbour, the propulsion units can be entered by engineers and electricians for routine checks.

Three bow thrusters, each of them providing a power of up to 2.2 megawatts at up to 300 rotations per minute, allow the ship to be steered only by adjusting the angle and the speed of the pods and bow thrusters, without using a steering gear. The propellers are mounted in front of the azipods for maximum propulsive efficiency. Each of the propellers features four fixed nickel-aluminium-bronze alloy blades which are bolted together and measure 5.5 metres in diameter. Each propeller blade weighs 4,800 kg and is held together by eight bolts. The maximum speed of *Queen Elizabeth* is about 24.3 knots and her cruising speed ranges between 18 to 21.7 knots. At maximum speed, the fuel consumption is approximately 9,800 litres of heavy oil per hour. It takes approximately six and a half minutes or a distance of 1.85 kilometres to stop the ship when it is cruising at a speed of 21 knots. A pair of Fincantieri Riva Trigoso stabilisers, one each on every side with an approximately 20 square metre fin, reduces the ship's oscillatory motions at rough sea. Two anchors provide the necessary stability when the ship is at anchor. An additional spare anchor is available on board too.

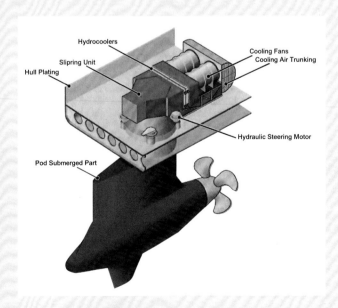

Das Wrack der *Queen Elizabeth* lag zwei Jahre im Hafen von Hongkong.

The wreck of *Queen Elizabeth* remained in Hong Kong harbour for nearly two years.

Beim Stapellauf am 20. September 1967 rutschte die *QE 2* so langsam von den Helgen, dass britische Zeitungen sie »Lazy Lizzie« – »faules Lieschen« tauften (unten).

Because of the slow sliding speed during the launch of *QE2* on 20th September 1967, the British newspapers named the ship »Lazy Lizzie« (bottom).

AUF ZU NEUEN UFERN: KREUZFAHRTREISEN MIT DER *QUEEN ELIZABETH 2*

Kein anderes Passagierschiff war wohl so populär, so elegant und so beliebt wie die *Queen Elizabeth 2* zu ihrer Zeit. Mit ihr hatte sich Cunard neuen Zielen zugewandt: Neben ihren Aufgaben im regelmäßigen Liniendienst sollte die *QE 2* auch als reines Kreuzfahrtschiff eingesetzt werden. Wichtiges Kriterium hierfür war ihre Größe. Mit 292 Metern Länge, 32 Meter Breite und einer BRZ von 70 327 passte sie durch die Schleusen des Panamakanals.

Am 5. Juli 1965 wurde auf der Werft John Brown am Clyde der Kiel für die Baunummer 736 gelegt – es sollte für diese Werft, die so viel mit Cunard verband, der letzte große Bau sein. Das neue Schiff brach mit vielen alten Konventionen: Statt gediegenem Holz kam großflächig Kunststoff zum Einsatz, knallige Farben und Dekorationen riefen bei älteren Passagieren bestenfalls Kopfschütteln hervor, Aluminium sorgte bei den Aufbauten für weniger Gewicht und die hochgelegenen Restaurants mit Seeblick für ein völlig neues Raumgefühl. Trotz dieser Neuerungen war die *QE 2* stilvoll bis ins Detail und Garant für elegante Reisen auf höchstem Niveau – nicht umsonst hatten sich Scouts schon Jahre vorher bei Mitbewerben im luxuriösen Segment umgesehen und spezifische Umfragen nach den Wünschen der Passagiere gestartet.

Der Name blieb bis zuletzt ein Geheimnis, Cunard Line hatte zunächst erneut *Queen Elizabeth* vorgesehen, doch Taufpatin Königin Elizabeth II. änderte bei der Zeremonie am 20. September 1967 eigenmächtig den ursprünglich vorgesehenen Namen in ihren eigenen: Queen Elizabeth, the Second.

Die Karriere des Ausnahmeschiffs begann alles andere als glanzvoll: Bei Probefahrten im November 1968 brach eine Schaufel in der Turbinenanlage, der Grund waren Materialfehler in den Aluminiumblättern. Erst im Mai 1969 war die Maschine wieder hergestellt, und das Schiff brach zu seiner ersten Reise nach New York auf, wo es am 7. Mai begeistert empfangen wurde.

Die Maschine blieb ein Schwachpunkt; auf einer Karibikreise im Jahre 1974 kam es gar zu einem kompletten Ausfall – alle 1600 Passagiere mussten evakuiert werden. Die norwegische *Sea Venture* kam zu Hilfe und brachte die Gäste nach New York zurück. Auch sonst verlief das Leben der

NEW MARKETS: CRUISING WITH *QUEEN ELIZABETH 2*

During her 41 years of service, she was popular like no other passenger ship of her time: *Queen Elizabeth 2* was the last true ocean liner, on icon of elegant travel at the highest level. Already in 1961, Cunard Line had undertaken surveys among the passengers of *Queen Elizabeth,* asking them their wishes: what they would like to have on board a new luxury liner? The Cunard teams travelled to luxury hotels all over the world and on luxury liners of other companies in order to ascertain the guests' taste for luxury. The new ship was intended to be used for the scheduled Atlantic service as well as a cruise ship, equipped to pass through the Panama Canal, with a length of 292 metres, 32 metres beam and a registered tonnage of 70,327.

On 5th July 1965, the keel for hull number 736 was laid at the John Brown shipyard on the Clyde. It was the last big order for this old-established shipyard. The new ship defied many old conventions: instead of solid wood, large areas were covered by synthetic material. The use of gaudy colours and decorations was disapproved and resented by the older passengers. Aluminium was used for the superstructures which resulted in less weight. The restaurants at a higher level offered sea views and a completely new sense of space.

The name remained a secret until the very last moment. Initially, Cunard Line had planned to name the ship *Queen Elizabeth*. However at the ceremony on 20th September 1967, her Majesty Queen Elizabeth II changed the originally planned name into her own, »Queen Elizabeth, the Second«, which stunned the Cunard management. This exceptional ship had a no glamorous start. During trial runs in November 1968, a blade in the turbine plant broke away. This was caused by a material fault in the aluminium blades. In May 1969 the engine was finally repaired and the ship departed for her first voyage to New York, where it received a warm welcome on 7th May.

The engine remained the weakest element, resulting in a total breakdown during a Caribbean voyage in 1974. All 1,600 passengers had to be evacuated. The Norwegian *Sea Venture* had rushed to rescue the guests and took them back to New York. Two years before, there had been a bomb

QE 2 alles andere als ereignislos: Zwei Jahre vorher hatte es eine Bombendrohung gegeben, als sich der Luxusliner mitten auf dem Atlantik befand. Die Passagiere bekamen erst mit, dass sich etwas Ungewöhnliches ereignet haben musste, als plötzlich ein Flugzeug der Royal Air Force auftauchte und vier britische Bombenexperten per Fallschirm landeten. Zum Glück fanden sie nichts. Der Erpresser, ein New Yorker Friseur, der 350 000 Dollar Lösegeld gefordert hatte, wurde vom FBI geschnappt und zu 20 Jahren Haft verurteilt. 1975 brach der Liner zur ersten Weltreise auf, 1982 trafen zwei Legenden auf der Atlantikstrecke aufeinander: die QE 2 und die Concorde. Im selben Jahr requirierte die britische Regierung die Queen Elizabeth 2 – ab dem 3. Mai sollte sie als Truppentransporter für den Falkland-Krieg dienen. Innerhalb weniger Tage wurde das Schiff für 3200 Soldaten umgebaut und grau gestrichen, am 12. Mai ging die 5. Infanteriebrigade an Bord, und nach nur 15 Tagen wurden Truppen und Material abgesetzt sowie 640 Verwundete von drei versenkten britischen Kriegsschiffen aufgenommen. Letztendlich entschieden die von der *Queen Elizabeth 2* angelandeten Truppen den Falkland-Krieg, in dem 655 Argentinier und 236 Briten ihr Leben ließen.

Nach diesem Einsatz musste die QE 2 selbstverständlich umgebaut werden, eine Maßnahme, der sie sich in ihrer langen Dienstzeit des Öfteren zu unterziehen hatte. War der eigentliche Bau 1967 mit stolzen 72 Millionen US-Dollar schon nicht ganz billig gewesen, investierte die Reederei während der 40-jährigen Fahrtzeit des Schiffes ungefähr das 15-Fache in Reparaturen und Renovierungen. Alles Investitionen, die sich lohnten: Nur so konnte die *Queen Elizabeth 2* ihren legendären Ruf als elegante, stolze und zeitgleich moderne Schönheit über die gesamte Zeit bewahren.

Hatte Cunard mit der QE 2 schon bei den Reiserouten Neuland angestrebt, so setzte die Reederei diese modernen Gedanken auch in der Technik um, als sie beispielsweise im Okto-

threat, as the ship was cruising on the middle of the Atlantic. The passengers were unaware that something unusual had happened, until an aircraft of the Royal Air Force appeared and four British bomb experts were dropped by parachute. Fortunately nothing was found. The blackmailer, a New York-based hairdresser, who had demanded a ransom of 350,000 dollars, was captured by the FBI and sentenced to 20 years imprisonment. In 1975, the liner took off on her first world voyage. In 1982 two legendary contructions, QE 2 and *Concorde* aircraft were serving the Atlantic route. In the same year on 3rd May, the British government commandeered *Queen Elizabeth 2* to use her as a troop carrier in the Falklands War. Within a few days, the ship was refitted to accommodate 3,200 soldiers and painted grey. On 12th May the 5th Infantry Division went aboard. After 15 days the troops and their equipment landed on the Falkland Islands. 640 combat casualties from three sunk British warships were taken on board. The troops that were dropped from *Queen Elizabeth 2* turned the course of the Falklands War. 655 Argentines and 236 Brits had ost their lives in this conflict.

During her years of service, QE 2 was consistently renewed and upgraded. The original cost building her in 1967 amounted to more than 72 million US dollars. In total, the shipping company invested approximately more than 15 times that for repair and refitting operations during her 40-year operation.

In October 1986, the last Cunard steamship set off on an Atlantic crossing. After this voyage, the steam turbine plant was replaced with modern diesel-electric engines within 179 days at the Lloyd yard in Bremerhaven. This 320 million Deutsch mark replacement brought an end to the era of steam shipping forever. The new drive resulted in energy savings of approximately 40 percent. Furthermore it resulted in a new top speed of 34.5 knots too.

In September 1995, the Queen survived a 30 metre monster wave caused by the hurricane »Luis«. The top of the waves had reached the bottom of the navigation bridge. Captain Warwick, who had seen the huge wave coming, said »It was a feeling as if QE 2 was running straight into the White Cliffs of Dover.« Apart from a fracture of an arm, several contusions, damaged furniture and a number of broken dishes, nothing inside the ship was affected. Only the railing on the fore ship was bent and some deck plates at the bow were slightly dented.

ber 1986 den alten Dampfturbinenantrieb aus- und die inzwischen weit zeitgemäßeren Dieselelektromotoren einbauen ließ. Eine Ära war zu Ende. Doch die Umrüstung, die 320 Millionen Mark kostete, bei Lloyd in Bremerhaven durchgeführt wurde und 179 Tage Werftaufenthalt bedeutete, hatte sich gelohnt: Trotz erheblicher Energieeinsparung durch den neuen Antrieb, gelang mit 34,5 Knoten eine noch nie da gewesene Höchstgeschwindigkeit auf einer Queen.

Andere Werftaufenthalte waren eher ungeplant: Als die Königin im September 1995 die Ausläufer des Hurrikan »Luis« kreuzte, überstand das Schiff diese Begegnung zwar einigermaßen glimpflich, aber doch nicht unbeschadet: Eine rund 30 Meter hohe Monsterwelle traf das Schiff, die Spitze des Wellengebirges reichte bis an die Unterseite der Brücke. Kapitän Warwick, der den gigantischen Wasserberg herannahen sah, meinte »es war, als ob die QE 2 direkt in die Kreidefelsen von Dover gefahren sei.« Bis auf einen Armbruch, mehrere Prellungen, beschädigte Möbel und viel zerbrochenes Geschirr wurde im Schiffsinnern nichts in Mitleidenschaft gezogen. Lediglich die Reling am Vorschiff wurde verbogen, und einige Deckplatten am Bug waren leicht eingedrückt.

Weltweite Aufmerksamkeit der anderen Art erhielt auch die Weltpremiere des Maybach, der im Juli 2002 auf der Queen Elizabeth 2 nach New York gebracht wurde. Der Daimler-Chrysler-Konzern hatte nach 60 Jahren die Superluxus-Marke mit dem Modell »Maybach 62« wiederbelebt. Während der sechstägigen Überfahrt stand das 360 000,– Euro teure Automobil in einem Glascontainer an Deck. Bei der Ankunft in New York holte ein Lastenhubschrauber die tonnenschwere Fracht vom Deck des sich noch in Fahrt befindlichen Schiffes an Land.

Worldwide attention was also caused by the world première of a Maybach, which was to be shipped to New York on board the Queen Elizabeth 2 in July 2002. After 60 years, the Daimler-Chrysler group had revitalised the super luxury brand by launching the model »Maybach 62«. During the six day voyage, the 360,000 Euro motorcar was stored in a glass container on deck. On arrival at New York, a cargo helicopter lifted the heavy cargo from the deck of the running ship and brought it ashore. Four passengers were so impressed by this Maybach motorcar, that they had already signed purchase contracts during the voyage itself.

On 18th June 2007, Cunard Line announced the sale of the Queen Elizabeth 2 for 100 million US dollar to Dubai World. Dubai World was constructing an artificial island, »The Palm Jumeirah« directly off the coast of the Emirates. QE 2 was planned to be moored alongside a specially built pier and she was intended to become one of the tourist attractions as a floating luxury hotel, a conference centre and a Cunard-Museum. the engine room would have to be completely removed in order to build a theatre for 500 spectators. When the last voyage of the ship on 11th November 2008 from Southampton to Dubai was announced, the shipping company set a new record: the last voyage of Queen Elizabeth 2 was fully booked within 36 minutes.

On 26th November 2008, the Queen reached her final destination. At present, however, the ship is still berthed fully functional in Port Rashid, as the global financial crisis has also left its marks on wealthy Dubai. Whether the reconstruction activities will happen, is still unknown. There have been several rumours, that the ocean liner was up

Vier Passagiere waren vom Maybach so begeistert, dass sie bereits während der Reise Kaufverträge unterzeichneten.

Rund 30 Jahre nach der Taufe gab Cunard Line am 18. Juni 2007 den Verkauf der *Queen Elizabeth 2* bekannt. Für 100 Millionen US-Dollar wurde das Schiff an Dubai World übergeben, die durch den Bau einer künstlichen Insel vor dem Emirat in aller Munde war. Der Luxusliner soll fortan als ein weiterer Höhepunkt, als schwimmendes Luxushotel, Tagungsstätte und Cunard-Museum dienen. Zudem soll der Maschinenraum entkernt werden und fortan ein Theater für 500 Zuschauer beherbergen. Nachdem dies bekannt wurde, geriet der Verkauf der Tickets für die letzte Reise der *QE 2* zu einem erneuten Rekord für Cunard: Binnen 36 Minuten war die 16-tägige Reise von Southampton nach Dubai ausverkauft.

Am 26. November 2008 machte die Königin an ihrem vorerst letzten Hafen fest. Dort ist das Schiff vorerst immer noch und voll funktionstüchtig zu sehen – die weltweite Finanzkrise hat selbst im reichen Dubai Spuren hinterlassen. Ob die Umbauten verwirklicht werden, ist momentan nicht absehbar. Mehrfach gab es Gerüchte, dass der Ozeanliner zum

for sale, but there seem to have been no serious negotiations so far. Only one inquiry from the South-African government can be confirmed. The Minister of Tourism, Martinus van Schalkwyk, had intended to transfer *QE 2* for 18 months to Cape Town in order to use the ship as a hotel during the football world cup. However, the worldwide demand for tickets before the event did not meet FIFA's expectations. So there was no shortage of hotel beds and consequently *Queen Elizabeth 2* remained in her new home port in Dubai.

During her active service, *Queen Elizabeth 2* set a world record for passenger ships, having sailed more than 5.9 million nautical miles and having carried more than 2.5 million passengers. The record holder had completed 806 transatlantic voyages from Southampton to New York in total (there and back) as well as 26 world voyages. After 41 years, 2 months and 7 days, this liner held the title of the longest-serving ship in the 171-year history of the Cunard Line. Today *Queen Elizabeth 2* is a floating legend having carried on board many prominent guests, including Queen Elizabeth II., her mother Queen Mum, Prince

Verkauf stünde, aber bislang hat es wohl keine ernsthaften Verhandlungen gegeben. Einzig eine Anfrage der südafrikanischen Regierung ist bekannt: Tourismusminister Martinus van Schalkwyk wollte die *QE 2* für 18 Monate nach Kapstadt holen und während der Fußball-Weltmeisterschaft als Hotel einsetzen. Doch da die Eintrittskarten im Vorfeld der WM weltweit nicht einen so reißenden Absatz fanden wie von der FIFA erwartet, blieb auch die prognostizierte Kapazitätslücke bei Hotelbetten aus und die *Queen Elizabeth 2* im neuen Heimathafen.

Im aktiven Dienst hat die *Queen Elizabeth 2* mit mehr als 5,9 Millionen Seemeilen einen Weltrekord für Passagierschiffe aufgestellt und dabei mehr als 2,5 Millionen Passagiere befördert. Insgesamt 806 Transatlantikreisen von Southampton nach New York und umgekehrt sowie 26 Weltreisen absolvierte die Rekordregentin. Mit 41 Jahren, 2 Monaten und 7 Tagen ist der letzte Liner das am längsten eingesetzte Schiff in der 171-jährigen Geschichte von Cunard Line. Mit der *Queen Elizabeth 2* geht eine schwimmende Legende für immer vor Anker, die viele Prominente als Gäste hatte, unter anderem Queen Elizabeth II., ihre Mutter Queen Mum, Prince Philip, den britischen Thronfolger Prince Charles, Lady Di, Prince Edward, Nelson Mandela, George Bush und Shimon Peres. Auch Künstler wie Paul McCartney, David Bowie, Elton John oder Peter Sellers standen auf der Liste der VIP-Gäste. Der Musiker Mike Oldfield benannte 1980 sein Album *QE 2* nach ihr, und der österreichische Maler Friedensreich Hundertwasser verstarb am 19. Februar 2000 an Bord. Aber nicht nur die Berühmten liebten dieses Schiff mit seiner edlen Linie, dem langen Bug und dem runden Heck. Neben etwa 150 Gästen, die jedes Jahr auf Weltreise gingen, gab es zahlreiche Passagiere, die mehr als 30 Mal mit dem letzten Liner reisten – und natürlich die Rentnerin Beatrice Muller, die mehr als acht Jahre lang bis zum Abschied in Dubai Dauergast auf der *Queen Elizabeth 2* war.

QUEEN ELIZABETH: DIE TRADITION WIRD FORTGESETZT

Als Anfang des Jahres 2006 der Startschuss für den Verkauf der Premierenreisen der *Queen Victoria* fiel, hatte das Cunard-management eine klare Strategie vor Augen: Man wollte mittelfristig mit zwei Schiffen in die Zukunft fahren. Einerseits

Philip, the British heir to the throne Prince Charles, Lady Di, Prince Edward, Nelson Mandela, George Bush and Shimon Peres. Artists such as Paul McCartney, David Bowie, Elton John and Peter Sellers were also on the VIP guest list. In 1980, the musician Mike Oldfield named his album *QE 2* in honour of the ship. On 19th February 2000, the Austrian painter Friedensreich Hundertwasser passed away on board.

But not only the celebrities loved this ship with its noble skyline, the long bow and the rounded stern. She had approximately 150 guests, who took off every year on a world voyage. There was also a large number of passengers, who had travelled with his last liner over 30 times. The pensioner Beatrice Muller spent more than eight years as a permanent resident on board *Queen Elizabeth 2* until she said goodbye to the ship in Dubai.

QUEEN ELIZABETH: THE TRADITION WILL CONTINUE

At the beginning of the year 2006 the ticket sale for the premiere voyages of *Queen Victoria* started. The Cunard management had a clear strategy in mind: in the medium term, the company's future had to be based on two ships. The new Queen, still under construction, would serve as a pure cruise ship, and *Queen Mary 2*, the world's largest passenger ship as the only liner in regular Atlantic crossings. It was evident then that *Queen Elizabeth 2* could only be kept in the fleet at high costs. The new UN ship's safety regulations in the mandatory SOLAS convention (International Convention for the Safety of Life at Sea), which would come into effect in 2010, would have imposed enormous refit efforts. Furhtermore, these new regulations require a drastic reduction of natural wood on board of ships, in order to minimise the risk of fire. However, when *Queen Elizabeth 2* was built in 1967, many exotic woods were used both on the inside and the outside of the ship. All of these would have to be replaced by flame-retardant materials. For this reason, the company was on the lookout for an opportunity to bid an honourable farewell to *QE 2*.

The thought, that the Cunard legend would go into the hands of another shipping company, was unacceptable to the management.

Aufgrund ihrer eleganten Linien gilt die *Queen Elizabeth 2* bei vielen Schiffsliebhabern als letzter echter Ozeanliner.

Many ship lovers see *Queen Elizabeth 2* as the last true ocean liner because of her elegant lines.

mit der im Bau befindlichen neuen Königin, die als reines Kreuzfahrtschiff eingesetzt werden sollte, und andererseits mit der *Queen Mary 2*, damals das größte Passagierschiff der Welt und einziger Liner im regelmäßigen Atlantikdienst. Die *Queen Elizabeth 2*, so viel war damals klar, würde nur unter großen Kosten in der Flotte zu halten sein. Denn die für 2010 beschlossenen Regeln zur Schiffssicherheit der verbindlichen UN-Konvention SOLAS (International Convention for the Safety of Life at Sea) hätten gewaltige Umbauarbeiten zur Folge gehabt. Die neue Verordnung sah unter anderem vor, den Anteil von echtem Holz auf Schiffen drastisch zu reduzieren, um die Brandgefahr zu minimieren. Da beim Bau der *Queen Elizabeth 2* 1967 aber innen und außen viele Edelhölzer verwendet wurden, hätten diese alle durch brandhemmende

Both Queens were performing well, but the advance bookings for the premiere season of *Queen Victoria* were so strong, that the company's management had to consider the immediate construction of another ship. Cunard Line intended to benefit from a continuously and fast growing market, especially in Europe. A further modern cruise ship only such as *Queen Victoria,* where the deck layout, interior and programme were tailor-made in accordance with the demands of cruise passengers, promised even bigger market shares. The planning efforts were intensified after 18th June 2007, when the Cunard Line officially announced the sale of *Queen Elizabeth 2* for 100 million US dollars to Dubai World and the termination of her active service. The liner's future being a hotel cum museum ship.

Das Bauschild der *Queen Elizabeth* weist die Baunummer 6187 aus.

Queen Elizabeth's name plate states her hull number as 6187.

Materialien ersetzt werden müssen. Darum suchte man einen Weg für einen ehrenvollen Abschied der *QE 2*. Dass die Cunardlegende für eine andere Reederei fahren würde, war für das Management ausgeschlossen. Mit den beiden Königinnen sah man sich gut aufgestellt, doch dann liefen die Vorausbuchungen für die Premierensaison der *Queen Victoria* so hervorragend, dass die Reedereiführung über den Bau eines weiteren Schiffes nachdachte. Cunard Line wollte damit von einem vor allem in Europa stetig und schnell wachsendem Markt profitieren, denn ein weiteres modernes, reines Kreuzfahrtschiff wie die *Queen Victoria,* dessen Deckaufbau, Ausstattung und Programm auf die Bedürfnisse von Kreuzfahrtkunden zugeschnitten ist, versprach noch größere Anteile.

Man sah sich nach einer möglichen Bauwerft um und stieg in Verhandlungen ein. Am 10. Oktober 2007 war es dann soweit, Cunard Line gab den Bau eines weiteren Luxusliners offiziell bekannt. Das neue Schiff sollte *Queen Elizabeth* heißen und seine Jungfernreise im Herbst 2010 antreten. Mit dem Bau wurde die renommierte italienische Werft Fincantieri betraut, die bereits die *Queen Victoria* abgeliefert hatte. Allerdings war diesmal in der Bauwerft der Victoria in Maghera in der Lagune von Venedig kein Platz, darum wurde die neue Queen am Standort Monfalcone bei Triest gebaut. Geplant war ein etwas größeres Schwesterschiff der *Queen Victoria* mit einer Bruttoraumzahl von 90 900 – damit ist es das bislang zweitgrößte jemals für Cunard in Dienst gestellte Schiff. Die Baukosten wurden mit etwa 410 Millionen Euro veranschlagt. Carol Marlow, damalige Präsidentin und geschäftsführende Direktorin von Cunard Line, verkündete voller Stolz den Neubauplan: »Die *Queen Elizabeth* wird in die großen Fußstapfen von zwei der bekanntesten Ozeanliner der Welt treten. Das ist für uns eine große Herausforderung und zugleich eine Verpflichtung. Diese neue Queen soll an die goldene Ära der Luxusliner erinnern und anknüpfen, mit vielen Art déco-Stilelementen und historischen Anleihen in allen Innenräumen bei gleichzeitig modernster Technik mit allen Annehmlichkeiten für die Passagiere. Mit der *Queen Elizabeth* wird die Reederei nach dem Ausscheiden der *Queen Elizabeth 2* im November 2008 wieder über drei Queens in der Flotte verfügen.«

Die Kiellegung war für den 2. Juli 2009 vorgesehen. Für die Design- und Werftteams von Cunard Line begann mit der Baubekanntgabe die zweite Planungsphase. Die äußeren Dimensionen des neuen Schiffs wurden mit 294 Meter Länge und 32,30 Meter Breite denen der *Queen Victoria* angepasst,

Cunard was looking for suitable ship-building yards and started negotiations. On 10th October 2007, Cunard Line officially announced their order for a new luxury liner. The new ship would be named *Queen Elizabeth* and its maiden voyage was planned for autumn 2010. The order was placed with the renowned Italian shipyard Fincantieri, where *Queen Victoria* had also been built. However at this time, *Queen Victoria's* building yard at Maghera, situated in the Venice lagoon, was fully booked. Hence the new Queen was commissioned to be built in Monfalcone near Trieste. The plan was to build a slightly bigger sister ship of *Queen Victoria,* measuring 90,900 RT, which would result in the second largest ship ever commissioned by Cunard. The building costs were estimated to be around 410 million Euro. Carol Marlow, former president and managing director of Cunard Line, proudly announced the new building plan: »*Queen Elizabeth* will follow in the giant footsteps of two of the world's most famous ocean liners. This is a great challenge for us and a commitment too. This new Queen shall remind us of and extend the golden era of the luxury liners, featuring many Art déco style elements and historical features in the entire interior, combined with state-of-the-art technology and utmost comfort for the passengers. After *Queen Elizabeth 2's* retirement from service in November 2008, the shipping company will again operate fleet of three Queens, once the new *Queen Elizabeth* will be available.«

The keel laying was planned for 2nd July 2009. This announcement marked the starting point for Cunard Line's design and yard teams for the second planning phase. The exterior dimensions of the new ship, 294 metres in length and 32.30 metres beam, were identical with those of *Queen Victoria,* but with 64.60 metres, the newcomer exceeded her height

mit 64,60 Meter ist der Neuling aber knapp zwei Meter höher. Außerdem sollte die *Queen Elizabeth* 36 Kabinen mehr bekommen als die *Queen Victoria,* sodass sie bis zu 2068 Passagiere befördern kann. Die zusätzlichen Kabinen waren für die Heckpartie vorgesehen, wodurch die Rückansicht allerdings sehr kastenförmig wirken würde. Der Tiefgang wurde auf acht

by almost two metres. Furthermore, *Queen Elizabeth* would have 36 cabins more than *Queen Victoria,* carrying up to 2,068 passengers. The additional cabins were planned in the stern area, giving the ship an extremely box-shaped appearance when viewed from aft. The designed draught was eight metres, and the hull was reinforced with steel plates, in order

Die Kiellegung fand am 2. Juli 2009 statt. Das erste der insgesamt 53 Segmente wog 364 Tonnen.

The keel laying took place on 2nd July 2009. The first of the 53 sections weighed 364 tons.

Meter ausgelegt und der Rumpf mit Stahlplatten verstärkt, um auch problemlos Atlantiküberquerungen vornehmen zu können. Damit war der Neubau so geplant, dass er gerade noch durch den Panamakanal passte, ein wichtiger Vorteil auf dem Kreuzfahrtmarkt. Das Projekt erhielt die Baunummer 6187, als Ablieferungstermin war Ende September 2010 vereinbart.

to allow for undisrupted Atlantic crossings. The newcomer's dimensions would enable the ship to pass through the Panama Canal, an important advantage in the cruise market. The project received the hull number 6187 and the delivery date was scheduled around the end of September 2010.

DIE OBERSTE GASTGEBERIN: HOTEL-MANAGERIN JACQUELINE HODGSON
THE HIGHEST RANKING HOST: HOTEL MANAGER JACQUELINE HODGSON

Eigentlich wollte sie nur 18 Monate auf See bleiben, doch der Job an Bord gefiel Jacqueline Hodgson so gut, dass sie seit 1978 auf Schiffen arbeitet: »Die Karrieremöglichkeiten sind hervorragend, und wo sonst hat man die Gelegenheit, Gäste aus so vielen Ländern und unterschiedlichen Kulturen kennenzulernen. Auf jeder Fahrt haben wir Menschen aus mehr als 40 Nationen zu Gast.« Ihre Karriere bei Cunard Line startete Jackie, wie sie an Bord genannt wird, in der Zahlmeisterei der *Queen Elizabeth 2.* Bis auf vier Jahre bei Princess Cruises blieb sie Cunard Line treu und stieg über zahlreiche Aufgaben und Positionen bis zur Hotelmanagerin auf. Neben dem Kapitän, seinem Stellvertreter und dem Chefingenieur ist sie nun einer der vier Senioroffiziere und Vorgesetzte von rund 850 Besatzungsmitgliedern. Der nautische Bereich, die Ingenieure und das Deckdepartment bringen es dagegen zusammen gerade mal auf etwa 150 Mann. Die Hotelmanagerin ist verantwortlich für nahezu alles außer Nautik und Maschine – die 1000 Kabinen, die Küchen, die Restaurants, die Bars, die Rezeption, alle öffentlichen Räume, die Lager unter Deck und selbst für die Abläufe im Krankenhaus an Bord, obwohl sie sich in den Kompetenzbereich des Schiffsarztes natürlich nicht einmischt.

Kaum ein Hotel an Land beherbergt so viele Menschen, rund 2000 Gäste und 1000 Angestellte, die nicht wie an Land das Hotel verlassen, um den Feierabend zu Hause genießen zu können. Hinzu kommt, dass bei nahezu gleichen Arbeitsabläufen der Platz auf einem Schiff wesentlich beengter ist. Mehr als 50 Nationalitäten befinden sich ständig an Bord, sie alle arbeiten und verbringen ihre Freizeit zusammen. Darum ist es für die Hotelmanagerin sehr wichtig, darauf zu achten, dass auch die Crew ein ausgewogenes Freizeitprogramm geboten bekommt. »Wir sitzen hier ja nicht nur sprichwörtlich alle in einem Boot«, sagt Jacqueline Hodgson, »das schweißt zusammen.« Die Moral der Crew hat für sie oberste Priorität: »Es ist wichtig, dem Einzelnen immer wieder Anerkennung und Lob auszusprechen und einen respektvollen Umgang miteinander zu schaffen, denn nur ein zufriedener Angestellter hinterlässt auch einen zufriedenen Passagier. Jeder ist gleich wichtig, wenn er seine Aufgabe gut macht. Auch der beste Koch könnte seinen Job nicht machen, wenn nicht beispielsweise der Gemüseputzer zuvor hervorragende Arbeit geleistet hätte.«

Neben Mitarbeitermotivation wird größten Wert auf Service und Komfort für die Passagiere gelegt, mit dem legendären White Star-Service hat Cunard Line einen Standard gesetzt. Die Reederei arbeitet weltweit mit ausgesuchten Personalagenturen zusammen, die nur ausgebildete Servicekräfte zur Auswahl vorstellen. Die von der Reederei Ausgewählten durchlaufen zunächst mehrere Wochen die Trainingscenter für den White Star-Service, die sich in Southampton, in Südafrika und auf den Philippinen befinden. Danach erfolgt ein intensives zweiwöchiges Training an Bord und der Einsatz in der Mannschafts- und der Offiziersmesse, bevor sie zum ersten Mal die Passagiere bedienen dürfen. Immer unter den wachsamen Augen der Hotelmanagerin und ihrer Bereichsleiter. Ein 16-Stunden-Tag ist für Jackie Hodgson nicht ungewöhnlich.

Sehr ungewöhnlich hingegen war ihr Einsatz für das Vaterland: Jackie war eine von 644 Freiwilligen, die sich für den Falkland-Einsatz der *Queen Elizabeth 2* meldeten. Innerhalb von 48 Stunden entschied sie sich im Mai 1982 für die Aufgabe, die 5. Infanteriebrigade mit 3200 Mann nach Südgeorgien und Verwundete zurück nach England zu bringen: »Ich fühlte, dass dies wohl die einzige richtige Gelegenheit in meinem Leben sein würde, etwas für mein Land zu tun.« Für ihren dreißigtägigen Einsatz wurde Jackie mit der Falkland-Medaille ausgezeichnet, sie ist die einzige der ehemals Freiwilligen, die noch bei der Reederei arbeitet.

Im Urlaub kehrt Jacqueline Hodgson in ihr Haus am Rande von New Forest zurück, das sie mit ihrem Ehemann bewohnt, den sie – wie könnte es bei einer so überzeugten Cunarderin auch anders sein – auf der *QE 2* kennengelernt hat.

Originally, she had intended to stay on board for only 18 months, but Jacqueline Hodgson fell in love with her job so much that she has been working on ships since 1978: »The career opportunities are excellent and where else do you have the opportunity to meet guests from so many countries and different cultures. On every voyage we have people from more than 40 nations.« Jackie, as she is called on board, started her career at Cunard Line in the purser's office of *Queen Elizabeth 2*. With the exception of working for four years at Princess Cruises, she has been with Cunard Line in various tasks and positions until she was promoted to hotel manager. With the captain, his deputy and the chief engineer, she is one of the four senior officers and a supervisor in charge of approximately 850 crew members. In comparison, the nautical, the engineers and the deck department altogether only have approximately 150 staff. Excluding navigation and engine room the hotel manager is responsible for almost everything: 1,000 cabins, the galleys, the restaurants, the bars, the front desk, all public rooms, the storage rooms below deck and even for the routines procedures in the hospital on board. Obviously she does not interfere with the doctor's work.

There is hardly a hotel on shore hosting so many people, approximately 2,000 guests and 1,000 employees. The staff cannot leave the hotel and spend the evening at home. Furthermore, the working space ist much more limeted on a ship. More than 50 nationalities are permanently on board. All of them spend their working and time off together. Therefore, it is very important for the hotel manager, to ensure that the crew is offered a well balanced leisure program. »Literally, we all sit in the same boat«, says Jacqueline Hodgson, »and this is good for the team spirit.« The moral of the crew is her top priority: »It is important, to constantly praise and acknowledge the crew's efforts, to create an atmosphere of respect for each other in order to and create a team spirit. Only a happy crew guarantees satisfied passengers. Everybody is equally important, as long as he does a good job. And even the best cook cannot perform at his best, if the vegetable cleaner has not done his job well.«

Apart from employee motivation, greatest importance is attached to service and comfort of the passengers, whereby Cunard Line has set standards with their legendary White Star Service. Trainees that have been chosen for the White Star Service attend serveral weeks at training centres based

in Southhampton, South Africa or in the Philippines. This training is followed by an intensive two weeks' training on board firstly in the crew's and in the officers' mess before they may serve the passengers for the first time, always under the supervision of the hotel manager and her division managers. A 16-hour day is not unusual for Jackie Hodgson.

Jackie Hodgson remarkably served her country onboard QE2: Jackie was one of 644 people, who volunteered to serve during the Falklands War on board of the *Queen Elizabeth 2*. In May 1982, she had decided within 48 hours to accompany the 5th Infantry brigade with 3,200 men to South Georgia and then bring combat casualties back to England: »I felt, this would probably be the only real opportunity in my life, to do something for my country.« Jackie was bestowed with the Falklands Medal for her 30-days service. She is the only member of the former volunteers, who still works for the shipping company.

Jacqueline Hodgson spends her time-off in her house close to the New Forest, where she lives with her husband. As may be expected from a passionate Cunarder, she has met him aboard the *QE 2*.

TÄGLICHE HOMMAGE AN DIE TITANIC: CHEFINGENIEUR ANDREW JONES

DAILY HOMAGE TO THE TITANIC: CHIEF ENGINEER ANDREW JONES

Andrew Jones kommt von der Isle of Man. Mit 16 Jahren begann er eine vierjährige Ausbildung bei den Isle of Man Steam Packet Company Fort Street Workshops, wurde übernommen und arbeitete anschließend weiter als Mechaniker und auf verschiedenen Werften des Vereinigten Königreichs. 1990 heuerte er bei Cunard Line an und begann als Ingenieur auf der *Cunard Countess*. Andrew machte Karriere auf der *QE 2*, der *Caronia* sowie der *Sea Goddess 1* und *2* und arbeitete sich hoch bis zum Ersten Ingenieur. 2003 wurde er dann zum Chefingenieur der *Seabourn Pride* ernannt und gehört seitdem zum Senior Officer Management, dem neben dem Kapitän und dem Staffkapitän, der Hotelmanager und eben der Chefingenieur angehören. Im Jahre 2005 wechselte er zum Flottenservice der Carnivalgruppe in Los Angeles, wo er für die Prüfung und Inspektion sämtlicher Schiffe der Reedereien P&O, Princess, Cunard und Seabourn zuständig war. Ab 2006 ging Andrew zurück auf See und wurde Chefingenieur bei Princess Cruises, wo er auf zahlreichen Schiffen arbeitete, ehe er 2008 zu P&O wechselte und auf der *Artemis*, *Oriana* und *Aurora* anheuerte. Die Rückkehr zu Cunard Line beschreibt Andrew als das wunderbare Gefühl, nach vielen Jahren mit Erfahrungen und Erlebnissen in aller Welt nach Hause zurückzukommen.

Der Chefingenieur hat in seinem Bereich insgesamt 19 Ingenieure, Elektroingenieure und Elektroniker als Offiziere, dazu kommen 55 Techniker, vom Schlosser, Mechaniker über den Elektriker bis hin zum Klimaanlagenbauer. Die Offiziere tragen goldene Schulterstreifen, die violett umrandet sind. Grund dafür ist ein Schiffsunglück: Als die *Titanic* versank, gingen alle Ingenieure mit dem Schiff unter. König Georg V. verfügte daraufhin, dass zu Ehren der Ingenieure Schiffsingenieure fortan violette Streifen tragen sollten.

Andrew Jones lebt allein und ist Mitglied des Institute of Marine Engineer's Scientists and Technicians. Seine Hobbys sind Oldtimer, Snooker, Heimwerken und Fußball schauen.

Andrew Jones comes from the Isle of Man. At the age of 16, he began his four years' training at the Isle of Man Steam Packet Company Fort Street Workshops. After that he worked as an engineer at different shipyards in the United Kingdom. In 1990, he was hired by the Cunard Line, and began his service as an engineer on board the *Cunard Countess*. Andrew made his career on board *QE 2*, *Caronia* as well as on *Sea Goddess 1* and *2*, working his way up to chief engineer. In 2003, he was appointed as chief engineer of the *Seabourn Pride*, and became one of the members of the senior officer management, which includes the captain, the staff captain and the hotel manager. In 2005, he went to the Los Angeles-based Carnival group fleet service, where he was responsible for the checkups and inspections of all ships of the shipping companies P&O, Princess, Cunard and Seabourn. From 2006, Andrew returned back to the sea and became chief engineer at Princess Cruises. He worked on numerous ships, before he changed to P&O in 2008. P&O employed him on board of *Artemis*, *Oriana* and *Aurora*. Andrew describes his return to Cunard Line as a wonderful feeling: coming back home after several years of various experiences and adventures all over the world.

In his department, the chief engineer is responsible for a total of 19 engineers, electrical engineers and electronics engineers in the rank of officers, as well as 55 technicians such as fitters, engineers, electricians and air conditioning technicians. The officers wear golden epaulettes, which are violet-bordered. The reason for this is a ship accident: when the *Titanic* sank, all engineers drowned. King George V decreed thereupon, that from then on ship's engineers had to wear violet-bordered epaulettes commemorating them.

Andrew Jones is single and member of the Institute of Marine Engineer's Scientists and Technicians. His hobbies are vintage cars, snooker, DIY and to watch football.

GEBURT EINER KÖNIGIN

A QUEEN'S BIRTH

Am 2. Juli 2009 lud Cunard Line ausgewählte Journalisten aus aller Welt nach Monfalcone ein. Auf der Werft waren mittlerweile die Blöcke so weit vorgefertigt worden, dass die offizielle Kiellegung stattfinden konnte. Die Zeremonie auf dem Fincantieri-Gelände stellte den vorläufigen Höhepunkt einer intensiven Gestaltungs- und Entwicklungsphase seit dem offiziellen Baubeginn dar. Vom wichtigsten strukturellen Einzelelement aus, dem Kiel, sollte das Schiff von nun an zu wachsen beginnen und bei Fertigstellung der Hülle aus insgesamt 53 Segmenten bestehen.

Im Rahmen der Zeremonie wurde das erste zentrale, 364 Tonnen schwere Segment, zusammengesetzt aus sechs Blöcken, von Lastkränen in das Trockendock hinabgelassen. Allein in diesem Segment waren bereits insgesamt 104 Tonnen Rohre, Kabel, Isolierung und andere wichtige Bestandteile verarbeitet worden.

Am 3. September 2009 wurde der erste Kapitän der *Queen Elizabeth* bekannt gegeben, der sich fortan als Werftkapitän mit einem Team von Cunard-Mitarbeitern auch darum kümmern sollte, ob beim Bau des Schiffes auch alle Vorgaben eingehalten wurden. Die Wahl fiel auf Christopher Wells, der 1992 als Zweiter Offizier der *Queen Elizabeth 2* zu Cunard Line kam.

Wells kannte sich mit Werftbedingungen und den anfallenden Aufgaben bei Neubauten bestens aus, denn nachdem er auf der *Queen Elizabeth 2* die Offiziersränge bis hin zum Rang des Stabskapitäns durchlaufen hatte, wurde er in das Werfteam für *Queen Mary 2* berufen und verbrachte 18 Monate im französischen St. Nazaire. Bei ihrer Indienststellung als Stabskapitän eingesetzt, wurde er 2008 zum Kapitän der *Queen Mary 2* ernannt.

On 2nd July 2009, the Cunard Line invited selected journalists from all over the world to Monfalcone. Meanwhile, the prefabrication of the blocks on the shipyard had reached a stage, that the official keel laying could take place. The ceremony at Fincantieri's premises was a symbol of the intensive design and development phase since the official start of the construction. Beginning with the most important structural component, the keel, the ship will start to grow from there, and on completion the hull will consist of a total of 53 sections.

During the ceremony, the first central 364 ton section, consisting of six blocks, was lowered by cranes into the dry dock. This segment alone housed a total of 104 tons of tubes, wiring, insulation and other essential components.

On 3rd September 2009, the first captain of *Queen Elizabeth* was nominated. From then on, he was entrusted with the task of supervising the construction on the yard, heading a team of Cunard employees and ensuring that all set standards would be adhered to during the construction of the ship. Christopher Wells, who joined Cunard Line in 1992 as second officer of the *Queen Elizabeth 2*, was appointed.

Wells was highly experienced and familiar with shipyard construction environment and all related tasks associated with new ship builds. He had been promoted from the normal officer's ranks on board *Queen Elizabeth 2* up to the rank of the staff captain. Then he was appointed to join the yard team for *Queen Mary 2* and he spent 18 months in St. Nazaire, France. He was staff captain on her commissioning and in 2008 he was appointed as the captain of *Queen Mary 2*.

It was a great honour for Christopher Wells when he became as the first captain of to helm *Queen Elizabeth:* »It will

Im Unterschied zu früheren Zeiten werden Schiffe heute nacheinander aus Segmenten zusammengesetzt. Besonders
gut zu erkennen: Fahrstuhlschächte und
Treppenhäuser (vorhergehende Seite).

In the past, first of all the entire hull was
built. Nowadays, ships are constructed by
assembling one section after the other.
The lift shafts and the staircases can be
clearly recognized (previous page).

Der Treppenaufgang des Britannia
Restaurants im Rohbau.

The staircase of the Britannia Restaurant
is structurally complete.

Christopher Wells empfand es als große Ehre, als erster Kapitän die *Queen Elizabeth* fahren zu dürfen: »Die *Queen Elizabeth* in ihren Heimathafen Southampton zu bringen, wird einer der schönsten Momente meines Lebens. So hoffe ich, dass die Bewohner Southamptons das Schiff so in ihre Herzen aufnehmen, wie sie es seit Indienststellung der *Queen Mary* im Jahre 1934 mit allen Cunard-Königinnen getan haben. Die *Queen Elizabeth* wird einer großen Tradition folgen.«

REKORD: JUNGFERNFAHRT IN EINER HALBEN STUNDE AUSGEBUCHT

Zwischen Planung und Bau blieb es knapp anderthalb Jahre zumindest äußerlich relativ ruhig um das Schiff. Zwar wurden in der Werft die Blöcke vorgefertigt, aber es gab in der Öffentlichkeit keine neuen Meldungen über das Schiff. Das änderte sich mit einem wahren Paukenschlag, als Mitte März 2009 der Buchungsstart für die Premierensaison der *Queen Elizabeth* für den 1. April um 14 Uhr mitteleuropäischer Zeit festgelegt

be one of the greatest moments in my life, to sail *Queen Elizabeth* to her home port Southampton. I hope that the citizens of Southampton will also hold this ship close to their hearts, as they have done with all the other Cunard Queens since *Queen Mary's*, commissioning in 1934. *Queen Elizabeth* will also follow a great tradition.«

RECORD: MAIDEN VOYAGE FULLY BOOKED IN HALF AN HOUR

After that, no news about the ship was disclosed for almost one and a half years. Although the sections were prefabricated in the shipyard, there were no further news about the ship in the public. This changed with a sensational bang when in mid March 2009, an announcement was made that bookings for the premiere season of *Queen Elizabeth* would be accepted from 1st April, 2 p. m. Central European Time onwards. Hundreds of blank cheques were sent to the shipping company's reservation centre. Cunard fans and ship lovers from all over the world wanted to be on board during her Maiden Voyage

wurde. Hunderte von Blankoschecks trafen in der Reservierungszentrale der Reederei ein, Cunardfans und Schiffsliebhaber aus aller Welt wollten unbedingt und um beinahe jeden Preis auf der Jungfernfahrt dabei sein. Insgesamt sechs Premierenreisen von Mitte Oktober bis Mitte Dezember sowie die Weihnachts- und Neujahrskreuzfahrt wurden bekanntgegeben. Der Start der Jungfernfahrt wurde auf den 12. Oktober 2010 terminiert, einen Tag nach der Taufzeremonie im Heimathafen Southampton. Nach nur neun Minuten waren die Suitenkategorien des Queens- und Princess-Grills vergeben, und es dauerte insgesamt nur 29 Minuten, bis die Jungfernfahrt restlos ausgebucht war. Auch auf allen anderen Premierenreisen war nur kurze Zeit später keine Kabine mehr zu bekommen.

Während einer feierlichen Zeremonie verließ die *Queen Elizabeth* am 5. Januar 2010 das geflutete Trockendock. Mit dem Aufschwimmen wurde die traditionelle Münzzeremonie durchgeführt. Auf italienischen Werften ist es Tradition, dass zum Aufschwimmen eine Patin, die sogenannte »Madrina«, ernannt wird. Als Madrina des Schiffes wurde die 79-jährige Florence Farmer ausgewählt. Ihr Ehemann, Willi Farmer, war

no matter what costs. In total, six premiere voyages from mid October until mid December including the Christmas cum New Year's cruise were advertised. The start of her Maiden Voyage was fixed to be 12th October 2010, one day after the naming ceremony at her home port Southampton. After only nine minutes, the suite categories Queens and Princess Grills Suites were fully booked and it took a total of another 29 minutes before the Maiden Voyage was completely full. A short time later, all the cabin categories for the other premiere voyages were also taken.

During a festive ceremony, *Queen Elizabeth* left the flooded dry dock on 5th January 2010. While the ship was floated out, the traditional coin ceremony was performed. It is a tradition at Italian shipyards, to nominate a special person for the floating-out procedure, the so-called »Madrina«. For this ship, 79-year old Florence Farmer was appointed as »Madrina«. Her husband, Willi Farmer, had joined Cunard Line in September 1938 as chief engineer and had served on board the first *Queen Elizabeth* as well as *Queen Elizabeth 2* until his retirement in 1979. During this coin ceremony, the new Cunard president Peter Shanks placed three coins

im September 1938 als Chefingenieur zu Cunard Line gekommen und fuhr bis zu seiner Pensionierung 1979 sowohl auf der ersten *Queen Elizabeth* als auch auf der *Queen Elizabeth 2*. Zur Münzzeremonie wurden drei Geldstücke von dem neuen Cunard-Präsidenten Peter Shanks als Glücksbringer unter den Hauptmast gelegt: eine britische Halbe Krone von 1938, dem Taufjahr der ersten *Queen Elizabeth,* ein Sovereign von 1967, dem Premierenjahr der *Queen Elizabeth 2,* und ein nagelneuer Sovereign von 2010 für das neue Schiff. In seiner Ansprache dankte Peter Shanks den Arbeitern: »Es sind gerade einmal sechs Monate seit der Kiellegung vergangen, und die Werft hat es geschafft, aus dem einzigen Stahlblock von damals im Dock dieses wunderbare Schiff entstehen zu lassen. In 170 Jahren Reedereigeschichte hat es mehr als 70 Jahre eine *Queen Elizabeth* gegeben, und dieses Schiff wird diesen Namen weit in das 21. Jahrhundert hinein tragen.«

Zum Abschluss segnete ein Priester das Schiff, dann wurden die italienische und englische Nationalhymne gespielt, und Florence Farmer ließ eine Flasche Prosecco an der Außenhülle zerschellen. Danach wurden die Schleusen des Trockendocks geflutet, und die neue Queen hatte zum ersten Mal Wasser unter dem Kiel.

Nach dem Aufschwimmen wurde die Queen Elizabeth vom Baudock an den Ausrüstungspier verlegt. Damit war die letzte Bauphase eingeläutet, vor allem die Innenausbauten wurden nun vorgenommen. Im Mai 2010 waren alle technischen Anlagen und Vorrichtungen eingebaut, und die Dieselgeneratoren konnten ersten Funktionstests unterworfen werden. Auch die Inneneinrichtung war deutlich vorangeschritten, die Ausstattung aller Gesellschaftsräume war zu erkennen und die ersten

beneath the mast, as a symbol of good luck: a British Half Crown from 1938, the christening year of the first *Queen Elizabeth,* a Sovereign from 1967, the first year of the *Queen Elizabeth 2*, and a brand-new Sovereign from 2010 for the new ship. In his speech, Peter Shanks expressed his thanks to the workers: »It is only over six months since the keel for this great ship was laid. In that short time, a solitary block at the bottom of the dry dock has grown into this awe-inspiring vessel. Of our 170 years of history, there has been an ›Elizabeth‹ in the fleet for more than 70 and this ship ... will take the name far into the 21st Century.« Then a priest blessed the ship, which was followed by the Italian and English national anthems. At the end, Florence Farmer smashed a bottle of Prosecco against the hull. After that, the locks of the dry dock were flooded and for the first time the new Queen had water under her keel.

After the floating-out, *Queen Elizabeth* was transferred from the building dock to the fitting-out pier. The last construction phase started especially fitting the interior. In May 2010, all technical equipment and appliances had been installed and the diesel generators had passed their first trials. The interiors and the furnishing of the saloons had already reached such an advanced stage, that the final finished state could be perceived. The first 500 cabins had also been put into place. Approximately 2,000 workers from 40 countries toiled day and night to build the new Queen in the docks. All the passenger cabin modules were installed in the beginning of July, paving way for the fitting out and furnishing of the cabin interiors.

Am fast fertigen Schiff werden nur noch letzte Innenausbauten vorgenommen (links).

The ship being almost finished; only final touches to the interior furnishings take place (left).

Aufbruch zur Probefahrt (unten).

Sea trial departure (bottom).

500 Kabinen waren montiert. Rund 2000 Arbeiter aus 40 Ländern bauten im Dock rund um die Uhr an der neuen Queen. Anfang Juli waren alle Module der Passagierkabinen eingefügt, sodass der Innenausbau der Kabinen beginnen konnte.

ZWEITE WELTREISE AB HAMBURG

Für viel Aufsehen sorgte die Bekanntgabe des Fahrplans der zweiten Weltreise der *Queen Elizabeth,* weil es eine historische Entscheidung war: Zum ersten Mal in der langen Reederei-Geschichte sollte ein Cunard-Liner nicht von der Britischen Insel, sondern von Deutschland aus auf Weltreise gehen. Hamburg wurde als Start- und Zielhafen für die Erdumrundung der *Queen Elizabeth* gewählt. Damit war die Hansestadt zum zweiten Mal Ausgangshafen für eine Premiere, denn der Fahrplan für die Jungfernsaison 2011, der von der Reederei bereits wenige Wochen zuvor vorgestellt wurde, enthielt eine Ostseepremierenfahrt ab/bis Hamburg. Am 3. Juli 2011 startete der Ozean-Liner zu einer Kreuzfahrt um das Skagerrak nach Skandinavien, Russland und ins Baltikum zurück nach Hamburg, wo die *Queen Elizabeth* am 13. Juli wieder eintreffen wird. Die Stationen dieser Reise sind Stockholm, Helsinki, St. Petersburg, Tallin und Kopenhagen. Bereits am Abend des 13. Juli wird die neue Königin die Hansestadt erneut verlassen und zu einer 14-tägigen Reise zu den norwegischen Fjorden und zum Nordkap mit Zielhafen Southampton aufbrechen.

Die 111 Tage dauernde Weltreise soll von Hamburg aus über Southampton nach New York, Fort Lauderdale, die Cayman-Inseln durch den Panamakanal nach Mexiko und die Westküste der USA führen. Nach San Francisco stehen Hawaii, Samoa, Fidschi und Neuseeland auf dem Fahrplan, bevor die Route von Sydney aus über Brisbane, Port Douglas, Kota Kinabalu, Hongkong, Chan May und Phu My (Vietnam), dem thailändischen Laem Chabang, Ko Samui, Singapur, Kuala Lumpur, Penang, Phuket, Colombo, Kochi, Mumbai, Dubai, Muskat, Safaga, Aqaba, Sharm-el-Sheikh, den Sueskanal, Alexandria, Piräus, Civitavecchia, Monte Carlo, Lissabon und Southampton nach Hamburg zurückführt.

Mitte August 2010 brach die *Queen Elizabeth* zu einer Serie von Probefahrten mit rund 600 Arbeitern und dem Cunard-Werftteam an Bord in die Adria auf. Drei Tage lang wurde während der ersten Fahrt auf dem offenen Meer bis Ancona die Technik mehreren Testläufen unterzogen. Dabei wur-

SECOND WORLD TRIP FROM HAMBURG

It was a great surprise when the schedule of *Queen Elizabeth's* second world voyage was announced on 14th July, because it was a historical decision: for the first time in the long history of the shipping company, a Cunard liner would not depart on a world trip from the British Isles, but from Germany. Hamburg was nominated as port of departure and destination for *Queen Elizabeth's* voyage around the world. This was the second time that the hanseatic city became port of departure for a premiere: the schedule for the maiden season 2011, which the company had already announced on 8th May, included a Baltic premiere voyage from and to Hamburg. On 3rd July 2011, the ocean liner will set off on a cruise around the Skagerrak to Scandinavia, Russia and the Baltic countries back to Hamburg on 13th July. The harbours visited during this voyage will be Stockholm, Helsinki, St. Petersburg, Tallinn and Copenhagen. On the evening of 13th July, the new Queen will leave the hanseatic city for a two week's voyage to the Norwegian Fjords and to the North Cape, ending at her home port Southampton.

The 111-day world trip: she will depart from the port of Hamburg, travel via Southampton to New York, Fort Lauderdale, the Cayman Islands, through the Panama Canal to Mexico and then to the US West Coast. The schedule will require the ship to depart from San Francisco via Hawaii, Samoa, Fiji and New Zealand before continuing further from Sydney. She will proceed via Brisbane, Port Douglas,

Auf der ersten langen Reise, Abfahrt nach Southampton (vorhergehende Doppelseite).

Ready for her first long voyage: departure for Southampton (previous double-page).

de vor allem das Antriebssystem überprüft. Die rund 40 vorgenommenen Tests zur Stabilität, Zuverlässigkeit und Leistung der Maschinen des Schiffes verliefen äußerst zufriedenstellend. Bremsverhalten, Stabilität und Manövrierfähigkeit der neuen Queen wurden durch Einschlagen eines scharfen Zickzackkurses mehrfach auf die Probe gestellt. Auch diese Tests verliefen erfolgreich.

Zurück in der Werft begann die letzte Ausstattungsphase, in den Passagierkabinen wurden Möbel aufgestellt: für die öffentlichen Räume wie Restaurants und Bars Stühle und Sessel geliefert. Die großen Kronleuchter im Britannia Restaurant und Queens Room wurden ebenso angebracht wie die letzten Kacheln im SPA-Bereich.

DIE QUEEN WIRD TAUFPATIN

Nahezu seit der Bekanntgabe des Neubaus hatte vor allem die britische Presse spekuliert, wer das neue Schiff taufen würde. Einhellige Meinung der Medien: eine *Queen Elizabeth* kann nur von der Monarchin persönlich auf ihren Weg geschickt werden. Die britische Regentin Queen Elizabeth II. war bereits im Alter von 12 Jahren vor Ort gewesen, als am 27. September 1938 im schottischen Clydebank die erste *Queen Elizabeth* von ihrer Mutter, ihrer Königlichen Hoheit Queen Elizabeth, getauft wurde. Das Cunard-Management hatte, der Tradition entsprechend, eine Anfrage an das Königshaus gestellt. Doch dies bedeutete nicht automatisch, dass die Monarchin persönlich die Zeremonie vornehmen würde. Denn bei der *Queen Victoria* wurde erstmals mit dem Brauch gebrochen, eine Cunard-Queen von einer britischen Königin taufen zu lassen; diese Aufgabe hatte das Königshaus für die Gattin des Thronfolgers Prince Charles, Camilla Rosear Mountbatten-Windsor, Herzogin von Cornwall und Rothesay, vorgesehen.

Um so stolzer war Peter Shanks, Cunard Präsident und Managing Director, als er am 1. September 2010 die Taufpatin der *Queen Elizabeth* bekannt geben durfte: »Die Taufe einer Cunard-Queen ist ein ganz spezielles Ereignis, und diese Taufe wird ein historischer Moment sein. Ihre Majestät Queen Elizabeth II. hat bereits 1967 Cunards *Queen Elizabeth 2* getauft und war 2004 zudem die Taufpatin des aktuellen Flaggschiffs unserer Reederei, der *Queen Mary 2*. Wir sind stolz und fühlen uns geehrt, dass ihre Königliche Hoheit auch bei der Taufe der *Queen Elizabeth* für eine dritte Cunard-Queen Pate stehen

Kota Kinabalu, Hong Kong, Chan May and Phu My (Vietnam), further onto the ports of Thailand viz. Laem Chabang and Ko Samui. From there, she will continue her voyage to Singapore, Kuala Lumpur, Penang, Phuket until Colombo. Then she will proceed to Kochi, Mumbai, Dubai, Musquat, Safaga, Aqaba, Sharm-el-Sheikh, and along the Suez Canal, to Alexandria, Piraeus, Civitavecchia, Monte Carlo, Lisbon and finally via Southampton conclude her trip back to Hamburg.

By mid August 2010, *Queen Elizabeth* had left for a series of trial runs with Cunard's yard team and around 600 workers on board to the Adriatic Sea. For three days during her first voyage at sea, the technical systems had to pass several test runs, before the ship finally arrived in Ancona. Specially the propulsion system was tested during this trip. The results of around 40 tests which ascertained the ship's stability, reliability and engine performance were extremely sucessful. The stopping distance, stability and the manoeuvrability of the new Queen were thoroughly tested several times by using a sharp zigzag course. These test results were excellent too.

After returning back to the shipyard, the final furnishing phase was carried out, and the furniture was installed in the passenger cabins. The chairs and armchairs were delivered and set up in the public spaces such as restaurants and bars. The installation of big chandeliers in the Britannia restaurant and Queens Room as well as the final tiles in the spa area brought the fitting out of the ship to a close.

LAUNCH BY THE QUEEN

Once the new build was announced especially the British press had speculated, as to who would be christening the new ship. The media were unanimous in their opinion: *Queen Elizabeth* should be christened by the monarch herself. When Queen Elizabeth II was 12 years old, she was present at the site on Scottish Clydebank on 27th September 1938, when the first *Queen Elizabeth* was christened by her mother, Her Royal Highness, Queen Elizabeth. Keeping in lines with the tradition, the Cunard management sought the consent of the British Royal Family. However, this request did not imply automatically that the monarch would indeed carry out the christening ceremony in person. *Queen*

Die einen nehmen Abschied, die anderen freuen sich auf die neue Aufgabe: Werftarbeiter und Cunard-Crew beim letzten Ablegen in Monfalcone.

Some say farewell, others look forward to a new job: shipyard workers and Cunard crew during her final departure from Monfalcone.

wird.« Die Taufe wurde für den 11. Oktober um 14.30 Uhr angesetzt, ungewöhnlich neben der Uhrzeit war der Wochentag, ein Montag. Der Grund hierfür lag in der Entscheidung des Königshauses, die royalen Experten der Klatschpresse mutmaßten sofort, die britische Monarchin wolle ihr Wochenende ungestört und in Ruhe verbringen.

ABSCHIED VON TRIEST

Währenddessen wurde die *Queen Elizabeth* in Italien auf der Werft für die Übergabe an die Reederei vorbereitet. Gemeinsame Teams von Fincantieri- und Cunard-Mitarbeitern gingen über das Schiff und nahmen alles genau unter die Lupe, um eventuelle Nachbesserungen vornehmen zu können. Die neue Queen wurde außerdem nochmal ins Trockendock verlegt, um den finalen Außenanstrich vornehmen zu können. Zu diesem Zeitpunkt befanden sich bereits 350 Cunard-Angestellte auf der Werft, der überwiegende Teil Techniker und Designer, darunter waren aber auch schon Mitarbeiter der Hotelabteilung, die ein Schulungsprogramm für die an-

Victoria was the first ship that did not follow this tradition, i.e. her christening ceremony was not performed by a British Queen. The Royal Family had designated Camilla Roseary Mountbatten-Windsor, Duchess of Cornwall and Rothesay, the spouse of the heir to the throne Prince Charles for her christening.

On 1st September 2010, Peter Shanks, Cunard President and Managing director, beamed with pride, when he officially announced that Queen Elizabeth II would launch the ship: »The christening of a Cunard Queen is a very special event and this christening will be a historical moment. Already in 1967, Her Majesty Queen Elizabeth II had christened Cunard's *Queen Elizabeth 2,* and in 2004, she also launched of our company's present flagship, *Queen Mary 2.* We are proud and very honoured, that Her Majesty will also be available for a third time, and christen the third Cunard Queen, *Queen Elizabeth.«* The christening was scheduled for 11th October, 14.30 o'clock. The time and the weekday (Monday) seemed unusual at first glance. However, the decision of the British Royal Family was not questioned at all. The experts dealing with Royalty from the Yellow Press

Cunard-Präsident Peter Shanks (ganz rechts) verfolgt stolz die Übergabe von Unterlagen während der Feierstunde auf dem Schiff.

Cunard's president Peter Shanks (far right) proudly watches the handing-over of the documents during the ceremony on board the ship.

reisende Besatzung erstellte und bereits die ersten Abläufe durchging.

Cunard Line enthüllte unterdessen am 20. September 2010 auf einer Veranstaltung in der National Portrait Gallery in London ein offizielles Porträt der Königin von England, welches die Reederei in Auftrag gegeben hatte. Damit wurde die Tradition, Skulpturen oder Porträts der englischen Königsfamilie auf den Cunard-Schiffen zu zeigen, auch auf der *Queen Elizabeth* fortgesetzt. Die Monarchin hatte der 31-jährigen Isobel Peachey aus Lancashire drei Sitzungen von je 60 Minuten Länge für das Ölgemälde gewährt. Der preisgekrönten, jungen Malerin war die große Bedeutung des Auftrags bei den ersten Gesprächen mit der Reederei überhaupt nicht klar: »Mir war zunächst gar nicht bewusst, wen ich malen sollte. Als ich erfuhr, dass es die Königin sein sollte, war dies sowohl ein Schock als auch zugleich eine wunderbare Überraschung«. Das Porträt zeigt Queen Elizabeth II. blau gekleidet, mit der Halskette von Königin Victoria und Ohrringen, die sie auch bei ihrer Krönung im Jahre 1953 trug, im Gelben Salon des Buckingham Palace. Der Präsident von Cunard Line, Peter Shanks, war voll des Lobes: »Isobel ist die jüngste Künstlerin, die jemals einen Monarchen malen durfte. Die Qualität ihrer Arbeit hat unser Vertrauen in sie belohnt, es ist ein wirklich wunderbares Bild Ihrer Majestät.« Das Gemälde war für die Grand Lobby vorgesehen und sollte an prominenter Stelle aufgehängt werden, an der Stirnwand gegenüber dem Café Carinthia auf Deck 2.

Die Übergabezeremonie des Schiffes von der Werft an die Reederei am 30. September fand vor kleiner Kulisse statt, das Hauptaugenmerk der Öffentlichkeit lag ohnehin auf der Taufe durch die Königin knapp zwei Wochen später. Nach der Ansprache wurde die italienische Flagge an Bord eingeholt und

speculated that her Majesty wished for an undisturbed and peaceful weekend before the event.

FAREWELL TO TRIESTE

The shipyard in Italy was preparing *Queen Elizabeth* for the hand-over to the shipping company. Joint teams of Fincantieri and Cunard employees inspected the ship and checked everything carefully, in order to carry out any necessary improvements. The new Queen was once again transferred to the dry dock, in order to receive her final exterior finish. At that time, there were already 350 Cunard employees at the shipyard, most of them technicians and designers. Amongst them there were also employees of the hotel division, who started on a training program for the rest of the crew and went through the first job routines.

In the meantime, on 20th September 2010 during an event at the London National Portrait Gallery, Cunard Line unveiled an official portrait of the Queen of England, which had been ordered by the shipping company. Herewith Cunard continued the tradition of showing sculptures or portraits of the English Royal Family on board *Queen Elizabeth*. Her Majesty spent three sessions of 60 minutes each for the oil painting with 31-year old Isobel Peachey of Lancashire. The award-winning young painter was unaware of the importance of the order during her first meetings with the shipping company: »At first glance, I was not aware, whom I should paint. When I learnt that it was going to be the Queen, it came both as a shock and a wonderful surprise to me.« The portrait shows Queen Elizabeth II dressed in blue, with the necklace of Queen Victoria and earrings, which she had worn during her coronation in 1953, in the Yellow Drawing at Buckingham Palace. The president of Cunard Line, Peter Shanks, was full of praise: »Isobel is the youngest artist, who was ever permitted to paint a monarch. The quality of her work is reflective of the confidence we had placed in her, it is certainly a wonderful portrait of Her Majesty.« The painting was meant for the Grand Lobby and would be hung in a prominent place on the front wall, opposite of the Café Carinthia on deck 2.

The hand-over ceremony of the ship from the shipyard to the shipping company on 30th September took place in front of a small audience, as the public were focussed on the christening ceremony by the Queen which was to take place

dafür der Blue Ensign gehisst, der seit 1864 die Dienstflagge Großbritanniens auf See ist und aus einem blauen Tuch mit der britischen Flagge, dem Union Jack, im linken Obereck besteht.

Noch am gleichen Nachmittag legte die *Queen Elizabeth* ab und nahm Kurs auf den Heimathafen Southampton, den der neue Ozeanliner nach 2949 Seemeilen acht Tage später erreichen sollte. An Bord wurde die Zeit genutzt, um die Besatzung weiter zu schulen und das Schiff auf Hochglanz zu bringen.

SOUTHAMPTON FEIERT DIE QUEEN

Im Heimathafen bereitete man sich auf die Ankunft der neuen Königin vor. Der Rat der Stadt hatte für das gesamte Wochenende von Freitag, 8. Oktober, dem geplanten Ankunftstag der *Queen Elizabeth,* bis zum Montag, 11. Oktober, dem Tag der offiziellen Taufe, ein umfangreiches Programm in der gesamten Stadt aufgelegt. Interessierte konnten sich im Maritimen Museum eine Ausstellung rund um die Cunard-Queens ansehen, im Archäologischen Museum wurden historische Filme zur ersten gezeigt, das Theater Guildhall Square spielte Stücke und Musik des elisabethanischen Zeitalters, der goldenen Ära der englischen Geschichte mit der Blütezeit der englischen Literatur wie den Werken Shakespeares. Kinder konnten sich mit Kostümen aus dieser Zeit verkleiden, Seemannsknoten und den Morsecode lernen oder Flaggen herstellen. Die Coverband »King of Queens« gab ein kostenloses Konzert der besten Stücke von »Queen«, und im Herzen der City wurde eine *QE 2*-Meile angelegt, ein Lehrpfad für Fußgänger. Außerdem wurden für Einwohner und Touristen Großbildleinwände aufgestellt, um auch denjenigen per Live-Übertragung das Verfolgen der Taufe zu ermöglichen, die nicht zu der Zeremonie eingeladen waren.

Am Morgen des 8. Oktober wurde die neue Cunard-Queen bereits am Eingang der Bucht gegenüber von Cowes von zahlreichen Segel- und Motorbooten empfangen. Vor den Eastern Docks sprühten Feuerlöschboote einen Vorhang aus Wasserfontänen und Tausende Schaulustige standen am Ufer und verfolgten gegen 9.30 Uhr das Anlegemanöver am Ocean Cruise Terminal. Auf dem Schiff wurde nach dem Einlaufen fieberhaft weitergearbeitet, um bis zum Eintreffen der ersten Gäste alle öffentlichen Bereiche und Kabinen vorbereitet zu haben, vor allem in den Küchen und Restaurants trainierte die

around two weeks later. After the speech, the Italian flag on board was lowered and the Blue Ensign was hoisted instead. The latter, since 1864 had been the ensign flag of Great Britain at sea. It is made of a blue fabric with the British flag, the Union Jack, in the upper left corner.

On the same afternoon, *Queen Elizabeth* set course to her home port Southampton, which the new ocean liner reached in eight days later having covered 2,949 nautical miles. The time on board was used for further crew training and highly polishing the ship to make her shine all over.

SOUTHAMPTON CELEBRATES THE QUEEN

In her home port, everybody was busy with preparations for welcoming the arrival of the new Queen. The City Council had planned an extensive programme in the city for the whole weekend from Friday, 8th October, the scheduled

Ankunft in der Morgendämmerung: zum ersten Mal im Heimathafen.

Queen Elizabeth's arrival at her home port in the early morning hours.

Crew Abläufe und testete die Funktionstüchtigkeit und die Kapazität aller Gerätschaften.

Ab Sonnabendnachmittag kamen die ersten Gäste aus aller Welt an Bord. Zur Übernachtung auf dem Schiff war ein ausgewählter Kreis von nur 900 Eingeladenen vorgesehen, neben der Führungsetage von Cunard Line waren dies Reeder und Manager anderer Kreuzfahrtlinien, die Führungskräfte von Partnern und anderen Wirtschaftsunternehmen, britische Politiker sowie die besten Reisebüropartner und Verkäufer und auch Journalisten aus aller Welt. Der Grund für diese Beschränkung war die Kapazität des Britannia Restaurants, wo nach der Taufe ein glanzvolles Galadiner stattfinden sollte. Direkt auf dem Kai neben der *Queen Elizabeth* waren drei Tribünen errichtet worden, hier sollten die Tauffeierlichkeiten stattfinden: eine für die Orchester und Sänger, direkt gegenüber die Ehrentribüne, vor der die Reden gehalten werden sollten, und eine Zuschauertribüne für insgesamt 2000 geladene Gäste.

TAUFE DURCH DIE KÖNIGIN

Zur Taufe der *Queen Elizabeth* am 11. Oktober 2010 erschien die britische Monarchin ganz in Blau und natürlich mit gleichfarbigem Hut. Standesgemäß ließ sich Queen Elizabeth II. gegen 15 Uhr in einem dunkelroten, klassischen Rolls-Royce

arrival day of *Queen Elizabeth*, until Monday, 11th October, the day of her official christening. Interested persons could visit an exhibition about the Cunard Queens in the Maritime Museum. The Archaeological Museum was showing historical films about the first *Queen Elizabeth,* the Guildhall Theatre was performing plays and music of the Elizabethan era, the golden era of English history with the zenith of English literature such as Shakespeare's works. Children could dress themselves up with costumes of that period, learning how to tie seamen's knots, learn the Morse code or how to make flags. The cover band »King of Queens« performed a free concert with titles from the best of »Queen«, and in the heart of the city a *QE2* educational trail for pedestrians was built. Furthermore, open-air wide screens were installed for residents and tourists, in order to provide live television of the christening for those, who were not invited to the ceremony.

In the morning of 8th October, the new Cunard Queen was already welcomed by many sail and motor boats at the entrance of the bay opposite of Cowes. In front of the Eastern Docks, firefighters boats sprayed a curtain of water fountains, and thousands of onlookers stood at the banks, watching the docking manoeuvre at the Ocean Cruise Terminal at 9.30 am. After her arrival, the the crew worked frenetically on board the ship, readying and organizing all the public areas and cabins before the first guests started coming on board. Especially in the galleys and restaurants, the crew was busy going through the job routines and testing the proper functioning and the capacity of all installed equipment.

On Saturday afternoon, the first guests from all over the world came on board. Only a group of 900 specially selected people had been invited for an overnight stay on the ship. They were members of Cunard Line's top management, and also ship owners and managers of other cruise lines, executive managers of partner firms and other commercial enterprises, British politicians as well as the top travel agency partners and their salesmen and journalists from all over the world. The reason for the limited number of guests was the seating capacity of the Britannia restaurant, where the invitees would attend a glamorous gala dinner, right after the christening ceremony. Directly on the quay next to *Queen Elizabeth*, three grand stands had been set up, where the christening ceremony was supposed to take place: one for the orchestra and singers, directly vis-à-vis the

Die Vorbereitungen für den großen Tag | The preparations for the great day are
sind in vollem Gang. Die Tribünen für | in full swing. The grand stands for the
die Taufzeremonie sind aufgebaut, die | christening ceremony are installed –
roten Teppiche fehlen noch. | only the red carpets are still missing.

vorfahren. Unter einem Baldachin wurde sie zunächst von den Stadthonoratioren von Southampton empfangen, dann begrüßte Cunard-Präsident Peter Shanks die Regentin und führte sie zu einem Besichtigungsrundgang über die Gangway an Bord. Dort wurde die Königin von Kapitän Christopher Wells empfangen und zunächst unter dem Applaus der Schiffsbesatzung durch die Grand Lobby zu ihrem Porträt geführt, wo die Monarchin das fertiggestellte Ölgemälde zum ersten Mal in Augenschein nahm. Danach begleitete der Kapitän Queen Elizabeth II. auf die Brücke, wo die Queen das Schiffshorn ertönen ließ.

Unterdessen hatten unten am Kai vor dem Schiff die geladenen Gäste ihre Plätze eingenommen, die Tauffeierlichkeiten begannen. Zur Eröffnung marschierten die Musikkorps der Coldstream Guards, dem ältesten Regiment der britischen Armee von 1650, und der Scots Guards über den Platz zur Showbühne. Nach diesem Auftakt spielte das Bournemouth Symphony Orchestra mit dem Symphony Chor unter Dirigent Anthony Inglis das Stück »Zadok, der Priester« von Georg Friedrich Händel, das seit 1746 bei jeder Krönungsfeier in Großbritannien gesungen wird. Danach erhob sich das Publikum und sang die englische Nationalhymne, denn Königin

VIP stand, in front of which the speeches would be delivered, and a grand stand to accommodate a total of 2,000 invited guests.

CHRISTENING BY THE QUEEN

For the christening of *Queen Elizabeth* on 11th October 2010, Her Majesty arrived dressed in blue with a matching hat. Befitting her rank, Queen Elizabeth II arrived in a chauffeur-driven classic dark-red Rolls Royce by 3 p. m. Under the baldachin, she was first welcomed by the dignitaries of the City of Southampton. Then the Queen was received by Cunard president Peter Shanks, who guided her over the gangway for a private sightseeing tour. On board, Her Majesty was welcomed by Captain Christopher Wells with great applause from the ship's crew. She was led through the Grand Lobby to her portrait, where the monarch unveiled the oil painting for the first time. After that, the captain accompanied Queen Elizabeth II to the bridge, where she blew the signal horn of *Queen Elizabeth* for the first time.

KREUZFAHRTDIREKTOR: ENTERTAINER UND PSYCHOLOGE
THE CRUISE DIRECTOR: ENTERTAINER AND PSYCHOLOGIST

Nahezu ihr gesamtes Berufsleben hat Amanda Reid auf See verbracht, im September 1977 heuerte sie auf der *Queen Elizabeth 2* als Dance Captain des Balletts an und stieg auf der Karriereleiter bis zur Kreuzfahrtdirektorin auf. Bereits mit vier Jahren begann sie eine klassische Balletausbildung, erwarb nach dem Schulabschluss ihr Diplom als Ballettlehrerin und tanzte danach drei Jahre für ein englisches Ensemble in London und Barcelona, bevor sie auf die *QE 2* ging. 1992 hängte sie ihre Tanzschuhe an den Nagel und arbeitete fortan als Social Hostess.

Neben zahlreichen Cunard-Schiffen wie *QE 2, Cunard Princess, Vista*- und *Sagafjord,* lernte sie durch Wechsel zu anderen Reedereien dabei auch alle Celebrity-Schiffe sowie die *Silver Cloud* und die *Silver Shadow* kennen. Doch 2004 verspürte sie »Heimweh nach der Cunard-Familie« und kehrte zurück auf das damals brandneue Flaggschiff *Queen Mary 2:* »Diese Reederei ist mit ihrer langen Geschichte etwas ganz Besonderes und so anders als andere Kreuzfahrtgesellschaften. Man ist stolz auf diese Tradition und lebt die alte Eleganz – das Gefühl des Reisens auf den großen Ozeanlinern – auch heute noch, die Geschichte wird weitergeschrieben. Das merkt man jedem einzelnen Cunarder an, und genau das lieben auch unsere Passagiere.« Nach ihrer Beförderung zur stellvertretenden Kreuzfahrtdirektorin im Juni 2006 ar-

beitete Amanda Reid während der Jungfernsaison auf der *Queen Victoria* und wurde 2010 zur Kreuzfahrtdirektorin ernannt. Ihre Lieblingsorte sind das Theater und der Queens Room, denn der klassische Nachmittagstee und die Bälle in festlicher Kleidung gehören für sie zu den Höhepunkten des Bordlebens: »Die Kleiderordnung ist sehr wichtig, weil dadurch dieses Gefühl von Eleganz entsteht. Auch viele junge Gäste lieben das, denn es ist deutlich anders als zu Hause. Ein Ball in einem Hotel ist nicht dasselbe wie auf einem Cunard-Schiff.«

Amanda Reid lebt in Kent und kümmert sich in ihrem Urlaub viel um ihre beiden älteren Tanten. Obwohl sie bereits die ganze Erde bereist und allein mehr als fünfzehn Weltreisen für Cunard Line hinter sich hat, liebt sie Städte- und Kulturreisen nach Prag, Florenz oder New York. Und auch an Land ist ihr die »Cunard-Familie« wichtig, sie trifft sich immer noch regelmäßig mit Freundinnen aus alten *QE 2*-Tagen.

Alistair Greener ist von früh morgens bis spät abends ständig präsent. Wenn Passagiere morgens das Bordfernsehen einschalten, verliest der Kreuzfahrtdirektor die Termine des Tages und interviewt Bordpersonal, Lektoren oder prominente Gäste. Vor- und nachmittags moderiert er die Einführungen zu Vorträgen der Lektoren und anderen Tagesaktivitäten oder veranstaltet die beliebten Quizrunden sowie Bingoturniere. Er ist Moderator der Abendempfänge, stellt die jeweilige Show im Theater vor, ist Gastgeber an einem der Ehrentische im Britannia Restaurant und ist überall zu finden, auch beim Tanzen auf den Galabällen im Queens Room.

Zu den gesellschaftlichen Aktivitäten kommen noch die administrativen Aufgaben. Denn der Kreuzfahrtdirektor ist Vorgesetzter von rund 120 Angestellten und verantwortlich für das gesamte Unterhaltungsprogramm an Bord, zu dem neben Theater- und Filmvorführungen alle Auftritte von Musikern und Schauspielern, das Gentleman Host Programm und sämtliche Veranstaltungen bis hin zum täglichen Sportprogramm gehören. Er ist neben den Hostessen einer der ersten Ansprechpartner für die Passagiere und muss neben Entertainerqualitäten auch über viel Menschenkenntnis und Fingerspitzengefühl verfügen.

Als Kreuzfahrtdirektor kann Greener seine beiden Hobbys Theater und Seefahrt ideal miteinander verbinden. Er verfügt über umfangreiche Fernseh- und Filmerfahrung und nahm unter anderem die Trainingsvideos für die Ausbildung des Servicepersonals für den White Star-Service auf. Aber auch an Land sind seine Fähigkeiten gefragt, das Mitglied der Britischen Schauspielergewerkschaft war in vielen BBC-Produktionen zu sehen und spielte im Warner Brothers Film »Black Beauty« mit.

Amanda Reid spent almost her entire working life at sea. In September 1977, she was hired on board *Queen Elizabeth 2* as dance captain of the ballet; soon she made a career for herself and finally she became cruise director. Already at the age of four years, she had begun classic ballet training. After finishing school, she gained a diploma as ballet teacher, followed by a three years dancing engagement for an English ballet company in London and Barcelona, before she came on board *QE 2*. In 1992, she gave up her dancing job, and started working as a social hostess.

Apart from beeing on numerous Cunard ships, such as *QE 2, Cunard Princess, Vistafjord* and *Sagafjord,* she had worked for other shipping companies too and had gained an insight in all Celebrity ships as well as the *Silver Cloud* and the *Silver Shadow*. But in 2004 she became »homesick for the Cunard family« and returned back on board *Queen Mary 2*, which at that time was the brand-new flagship: »This shipping company with its long history is something very special and completely different when compared to other cruise lines. One feels proud of this tradition and lives the old elegance – the feeling of travelling on board of these huge ocean liners is stimulating – and even today, the history continues and that is just what our passengers like.« After promotion to assistant cruise director in June 2006, Amanda Reid worked on *Queen Victoria* during the maiden season and became cruise director in 2010. Her favourite places are the theatre and the Queens Room, because the classic afternoon tea and the balls in formal dress are the highlights for her on board: »The dress code is very important, because this creates a feeling of elegance. Many young guests like that, because this experience is completely different from the one they have at home. A ball in a hotel is not the same as on a Cunard ship.« Amanda Reid lives in Kent. On holiday, she spends a lot of time with her two elderly aunts. Although she has already travelled

the world quite a number of times, including more than fifteen world trips for Cunard Line, she is still fond of city and cultural trips to Prague, Florence or New York. And even when she is shore-based, the »Cunard family« is very important to her. She still regularly meets friends from the old *QE 2* days.

Alistair Greener is always available right from the early hours in the morning until late in the evening. When the passengers switch on their TV after waking up, the cruise director reads out the programme highlights for the day and followed by interviews with the crew, editors or prominent guests. In the morning and afternoon, he announces lectures of the editors and other activities for the day. He is in charge of popular quiz games including Bingo tournaments. He is the presenter during the evening receptions and shows in the theatre. He is also the host at one of the top tables in the Britannia Restaurant. He can be found virtually everywhere, even dancing at the gala balls in the Queens Room.

In addition to the social activities, he is also responsible for administrative tasks. The cruise director is supervising 120 employees and is responsible for the entire entertainment programme on board, which includes the theatre and the cinema shows, all performances by musicians and actors, the Gentleman Host Programme and all events including the daily sports programme. The cruise director prepares the daily programme, which is made available in the cabins one night before, so that the passengers can decide beforehand, which films they would prefer to watch on the interactive TV the next day. Along with the hostesses, he is one of the main contact persons for the passengers and must not only possess entertainer skills but also lot of knowledge about human nature and diplomatic behaviour.

Before Alistair Greener recently changed to the newest Cunard ship, he occupied the same position on board of *Queen Elizabeth 2, Queen Mary 2* and *Queen Victoria*. As Cruise Director he can ideally combine both his hobbies – theatre and shipping. Greener has an extensive knowledge of TV and cinema. He not only produces the daily on-board TV programme, but is also engaged in the production of training videos for the White Star Service staff. His skills are also required on shore: as member of the British Actors' Equity, he has performed in many BBC productions and also starred in the Warner Brothers' film »Black Beauty«.

Die glanzvolle Taufzeremonie wird mit dem musikalischen Einmarsch der Guards eröffnet. Die Königin lässt sich unterdessen von Kapitän Wells die Brücke zeigen, bevor sie auf der Ehrentribüne neben dem Präsidenten der Cunard-Muttergesellschaft Carnival Corporation, Mickey Arison, Platz nimmt. Cunard-Präsident Peter Shanks hält die Taufrede, der Bischof von Winchester segnet das Schiff.

The glamourous christening ceremony started with a musical performance by the Guards marching in. Her Majesty was shown the navigation bridge by Captain Wells, before she took a seat at the VIP stand next to Mickey Arison, president of the Cunard holding company Carnival Corporation. Cunard's president, Peter Shanks, delivered the christening speech, and the Bishop of Winchester blessed the ship.

Elizabeth II. war auf dem Festplatz vorgefahren und wurde in die königliche Loge geführt. In seiner folgenden Begrüßungsrede sagte Cunard-Präsident Peter Shanks: »Es gibt nur eine einzige Person, die bei den Taufen von allen drei Schiffen mit dem Namen *Queen Elizabeth* dabei war und das sind Sie, Eure Majestät.«

Nach der Rede erklang »Amazing Grace« gespielt von den beiden Dudelsackpfeifern Louise Marshall Millington und Paul Young von den Coldstream Guards, die auf einer Bordklappe der *Queen Elizabeth* gleich neben dem Namenszug standen, hoch über den Köpfen der Zuschauer. In schwerem Ornat betrat der Bischof von Winchester, Right Reverend Michael Scott-Joynt, die Bühne und erteilte dem Schiff seinen Segen. Jetzt war der große Augenblick gekommen: Der erste Kapitän der neuen Queen, Christopher Wells, holte die Taufpatin aus ihrer königlichen Loge ab und führte sie auf das Podium. Die Königin trat ans Rednerpult und sagte mit fester Stimme: »Ich taufe dieses Schiff auf den Namen *Queen Elizabeth*. Gott schütze sie und alle, die mit ihr fahren.« Dann drückte die Königin einen Knopf und ließ, gemäß der Cunard-Tradition keinen Champagner, sondern Weißwein zu verwenden, eine Magnumflasche Rothschild Cunard Graves des Jahrgangs 2009 am Bug zerschellen. Dazu schmetterten die Trompeter der Irish Guards die Fanfare von Cunard Line.

Zu den anschließenden Klängen von »Pomp and Circumstance« erhob sich Queen Elizabeth II. und verließ die Zere-

In the meantime, the invited guests had taken their seats at the quay next to the ship's bow, and the christening ceremony began. The grand opening started with the marching of the music corps of the Coldstream Guards, the oldest regiment of the British Army from 1650, and the Scots Guards over the square to the show stage. After this prelude, the Bournemouth Symphony Orchestra and the Symphonic Choir performed the composition »Zadok, the priest« by Georg Friedrich Händel, conducted by Anthony Inglis, which has been sung at every coronation ceremony in Great Britain since 1746. Then Queen Elizabeth II made her way to the festivity area and was guided to her Royal Box. The people sang the English national anthem with a standing ovation. In the welcome speech which followed, Cunard president Peter Shanks emphasised: »There is only one person, who has attended the christening of all three ships bearing the name *Queen Elizabeth,* and that's you, Your Majesty.«

After the speech, »Amazing Grace« was played by the two bagpipers Louise Marshall Millington and Paul Young from the Coldstream Guards, who stood on a platform of the *Queen Elizabeth*, right next to the ship's name, high above the heads of the spectators. The bishop of Winchester, Right Reverend Michael Scott-Joynt, entered the stage wearing his regalia, and blessed the ship. Now the big moment was to come: The Master of *Queen Elizabeth,* Christopher Wells,

approached Her Majesty in the Royal Box and escorted her to the podium. The Queen stood at the speaker's desk and said with a firm voice: »I hereby christen this ship *Queen Elizabeth*. God will save this ship and all those who will travel with her.« Then the Queen pressed a button and a magnum bottle of Rothschild Cunard Graves, vintage 2009 (following the Cunard tradtion with white wine instead of champagne) was released against the bow. The trumpeters of the Irish Guards were belting out the Cunard Line's fanfare.

When »Pomp and Circumstance« was played, Queen Elizabeth II stood up and left the ceremony, waving towards the spectators. Finally, on behalf of the shipping company, Peter Shanks bade good bye to the guests of the christening ceremony: »This moment will continue to be the talk for many years to come as it is yet another historical moment for us. By departing on her Maiden Voyage, *Queen Elizabeth* will soon find her place next to her sisters *Queen Mary 2* and *Queen Victoria*. Cunard's present fleet symbolises the triumph of a great tradition.«

After the christening ceremony, the 900 invited guests took their seats for a gala dinner in the Britannia restaurant that lasted until the early hours of the morning. One day later, *Queen Elizabeth,* accompanied by some thousand spectators and dozens of boats, bade farewell with a grand display of fireworks at 5 p. m. She left for her two weekly Maiden Voyage to the Canary Islands.

In total six premiere voyages and the 23-day Christmas and New Year's cruise were on the schedule before *Queen Elizabeth* returned back to her home port on 5th January, in order to embark on her first world trip. The prelude was a voyage together with Queen Victoria across the Atlantic to New York, to participate in a rendezvous of all three Queens of the seas on 13th January.

monie, nachdem sie ins Publikum gewunken hatte. Zum Abschluss verabschiedete Peter Shanks im Namen der Reederei die Taufgäste: »Von diesem Augenblick werden Sie noch in vielen Jahren reden, denn dies ist ein weiterer historischer Moment für uns. Mit dem Aufbruch zu ihrer Jungfernreise wird die *Queen Elizabeth* den Platz neben ihren Schwestern *Queen Mary 2* und *Queen Victoria* einnehmen. Cunards derzeitige Flotte ist der Triumph einer großen Tradition.« Nach den Tauffeierlichkeiten fand an Bord im Britannia Restaurant ein Galadiner für 900 geladene Gäste statt, das bis in die frühen Morgenstunden dauerte. Einen Tag später brach die *Queen Elizabeth,* verabschiedet von einem Feuerwerk und einigen Tausend Schaulustigen und Dutzenden von Booten, gegen 17 Uhr zu ihrer 14-tägigen Jungfernreise zu den Kanarischen Inseln auf.

Insgesamt sechs Premierenfahrten und die 23-tägige Weihnachts- und Neujahrsreise standen auf dem Programm, bis die *Queen Elizabeth* am 5. Januar in ihren Heimathafen zurückkehrte, um ihre erste Weltreise zu starten. Den Auftakt bildete die Tandemfahrt über den Atlantik mit der *Queen Victoria* nach New York, wo es am 13. Januar zum Treffen mit der *Queen Mary 2* kam, dem Stelldichein der drei Königinnen der Meere.

TREFFEN DER DREI QUEENS IN NEW YORK

Auf den Tag genau drei Jahre nach dem allerersten Treffen von drei Königinnen in der Reedereigeschichte, der *Queen Elizabeth 2, Queen Mary 2* und *Queen Victoria,* kam es am 13. Januar 2011 erneut zu einem Rendezvous Royal in New

RENDEZVOUS OF THE THREE QUEENS IN NEW YORK

On 13th January 2011, exactly three years after the very first meeting of three Queens in the history of the shipping line, *Queen Elizabeth 2, Queen Mary 2* and *Queen Victoria,* there was another Royal Rendezvous in New York, this time with the new fleet member *Queen Elizabeth.* After the photos of 2008 rendezvous meeting spread across the world, the Cunard

Zur Feier des Drei-Königinnen-Treffens am 13. Januar 2011 läutet Commodore Bernard Warner mit der Schiffsglocke der ersten Queen Elizabeth zum Börsenschluss der New York Stock Exchange.

During a rendezvous of the three Queens on 13th January 2011, Commodore Bernard Warner rang the first Queen Elizabeth's ship's bell at the close of trading at the New York Stock Exchange.

York, dieses Mal mit dem neuen Flottenmitglied Queen Elizabeth. Nachdem die Bilder 2008 um die Welt gegangen waren, hatte das Cunard-Management noch vor der Fertigstellung der im Bau befindlichen Queen Elizabeth beschlossen, die Fahrpläne der drei Queens so aufeinander abzustimmen, dass wiederum ein Treffen auf dem Hudson möglich wurde.

Zwei Jahre hatten die Vorbereitungen für diesen Tag gedauert, der Plan musste von verschiedenen offiziellen Stellen genehmigt werden, neben der Hafenbehörde und der New Yorker Wirtschaftsbehörde schalteten sich auch Küstenwache, die New Yorker Polizei und sogar das FBI ein. Insgesamt 4000 Arbeiter wurden von Hafenbehörde und Dienstleistern bereitgestellt, um die Ozeandampfer zu entladen und zu versorgen sowie die Passagiere aus- und einsteigen zu lassen.

Zehntausende New Yorker säumten die Küsten Manhattans vom Battery Park bis zum Hudson River Park, um diesem Ereignis beizuwohnen. Während der majestätischen Feierlichkeiten, die durch 21 Salutschüsse eröffnet wurden, verließen die drei Queens am frühen Abend des 13. Januar in einem Prozessionszug den New Yorker Hafen. Zudem wurde das Empire State Building zur Feier des Tages mit gewaltigen Strahlern in die Reedereifarbe Rot getaucht. Micky Arison, CEO und Vorsitzender der Carnival-Gruppe, Cunard-Präsident Peter Shanks

management decided even before completion of Queen Elizabeth, to coordinate the sailing schedules of the three Queens, so as to accomplish another meeting on the River Hudson.

The preparation for this day took two years, as the plan had to be approved by different official bodies, including the New York port authority, the New York Chamber of Commerce, the coast guard, the New York police and even the FBI. In total 4,000 workers were made available by the port authority and further service providers, in order to unload and to provision the ocean steamers and to assist in the disembarking and embarking of the passengers.

Tens of thousands of New Yorkers lined up along the coastline of Manhattan from Battery Park to Hudson River Park to witness this event. During the majestic celebrations, which started with 21 cannon salutes, the three Queens left New York harbour on 13th January in the early evening on an outbound parade. Furthermore to mark this occasion, the Empire State Building was illuminated with huge spotlights in the company's colour: red. Micky Arison, CEO and chairman of the Carnival group, Cunard president Peter Shanks and the Commodore of the shipping company, Bernard Warner, had already rung

und der Commodore der Reederei, Bernard Warner, hatten zuvor bereits an der New Yorker Börse mit der Originalschiffsglocke der ersten *Queen Elizabeth* von 1938 die Schlussglocke erklingen lassen.

Die Auslaufparade der drei Queens wurde von Feuerwehr- und Polizeibooten begleitet, die Wasserfontänen sprühten und Lichtkegel vor dem Bug der *Queen Mary 2* erleuchten ließen, welche die Prozession in südöstlicher Richtung den Hudson hinunter anführte, gefolgt von *Queen Victoria* und *Queen Elizabeth*. Passagiere und Mannschaft standen dichtgedrängt und winkten von den angestrahlten Decks hinab.

Gegen 19 Uhr zündeten zwei Schlepper ein 20-minütiges Großfeuerwerk abgestimmt auf ein musikalisches Potpourri

the final bell using the original ship's bell of the first *Queen Elizabeth* of 1938 in the New York Stock Exchange.

The outbound parade of the three Queens was accompanied by boats of the Fire and Police Department, which sprayed water fountains and created light beams in front of *Queen Mary 2*'s bow which led the outbound parade in a south-easterly direction down the River Hudson, closely followed by *Queen Victoria* and *Queen Elizabeth*. Passengers and crew stood close together, waving excitedly from the illuminated decks.

At 7 p. m., there was a 20 minute long, magnificent display of fireworks, fired from two tugs off Liberty Island and Ellis Island. The aerial fireworks were coordinated with a med-

Die Auslaufparade mit großem Feuerwerk wird von der *Queen Mary 2*
angeführt (rechts vorn), dahinter folgen
Queen Victoria und *Queen Elizabeth*.

The outbound parade, accompanied by
a grand display of fireworks, was led
by *Queen Mary 2* (right, at the front),
followed by *Queen Victoria* and *Queen
Elizabeth.*

klassischer Melodien, welches auf allen drei Schiffen synchron abgespielt wurde und bestand fast ausschließlich aus den Farben Rot, Weiß und Blau, den Farben der Nationalflaggen Großbritanniens und den USA.

Zum grandiosen Feuerwerksfinale passierten die drei Queens die Südspitze Manhattans und kreuzten vor der Freiheitsstatue. Danach nahmen die Schiffe langsam Fahrt auf und fuhren nacheinander unter der Verrazano Narrows Brücke hindurch. Die *Queen Mary 2* steuerte im Rahmen ihrer fünften Weltreise Fort Lauderdale an, die *Queen Victoria* nahm Kurs auf den Panamakanal und die *Queen Elizabeth* setzte ihre erste, 103-tägige Weltreise mit Ziel Florida fort.

ley of classic melodies, which were synchronously played on all three ships. The colours of the fireworks' display were mainly red, white and blue. These three colours represent the colours of the national ensigns of Great Britain and the USA.

At the grand finale of the fireworks' display, the three Queens passed the southern tip of Manhattan and cruised in front of the Statue of Liberty. After that, the ships gathered speed slowly yet steadily, and passed under the Verrazano Narrows Bridge one after the other. *Queen Mary 2* was bound for Fort Lauderdale as part of her fifth world voyage, *Queen Victoria* set off on its course to the Panama Canal while *Queen Elizabeth* continued with her first 103-days world voyage towards Florida.

DIE BRÜCKE
THE BRIDGE

Die Kommandozentrale befindet sich auf Deck 8, ist 36 Meter breit und reicht damit auf beiden Seiten 2 Meter über die Breite des Schiffes hinaus. Über die Brückenflügel sind beide Seiten der *Queen Elizabeth* gut einsehbar – eine nicht zu verachtende Hilfe beim Anlegen für die Brückenbesatzung, weil sie so einen besseren Überblick hat. Um die Sicht noch weiter zu verbessern, sind selbst in den Boden beider Flügel große Glasplatten eingelassen. Der Steuermann hat freie Sicht direkt nach unten und kann so die Entfernung zu den Kaianlagen besser einschätzen. Auf beiden Brückenflügeln befinden sich jeweils Pulte mit sämtlichen Steuer- und Computerelementen, die auch auf den Kontrolltafeln in der Brückenmitte vorhanden sind, sodass das Schiff auch von hier aus manövriert werden kann. Mit einer Brückenhöhe von 26 Metern ist der Horizont ungefähr 18 Kilometer entfernt, durch ihre Höhe über der Wasserlinie sind andere Schiffe aber noch aus weiterer Entfernung sichtbar.

Die Brücke ist mit modernster Technik bestückt, das Herzstück bilden große Bildschirme in der Brückenmitte, auf denen die wachhabenden Offiziere sich elektronische Seekarten, Radarpositionen, Kollisionswarner und das Sicherheitssystem in unterschiedlichen Größen und Auflösungen anzeigen lassen können. Dieses System hat gegenüber Seekarten aus Papier mehrere Vorteile; es nimmt weniger Platz weg – auf der *QE 2* wurden rund 1800 Seekarten bereitgehalten – und die auf den Karten der Britischen Admiralität beruhenden elektronischen Karten sind immer auf dem neuesten Stand, das System wird automatisch wöchentlich versorgt. Für schwierige Passagen gibt es zusätzlich Seekarten aus Papier. Der Kartentisch, an dem auch junge Offiziere ihre Navigationskenntnisse üben, befindet sich auf der Steuerbordseite.

Ein GPS (Global Positioning System) errechnet die aktuelle Position. Zusätzlich bestimmt aber auf jeder Wache ein Offizier die Position anhand der Sonne oder der Sterne und vergleicht die errechnete Position mit der vom Kompass angegebenen, um eventuelle Abweichungen zu bemerken, denn der Magnetkompass wird durch das Magnetfeld rund um das Schiff mit seiner Stahlhülle und die elektronischen Geräte beeinflusst. Radarscanner und -prozessoren sorgen für Sicherheit auf See. Mit dem ARPA-System (Automatic Radar Plotting Aid) können bis zu 40 Objekte gleichzeitig auf den Bildschirmen verfolgt wer-

den. Kurs und Geschwindigkeit der erfassten Schiffe werden genauso angezeigt wie Distanz und Zeitpunkt der vorausberechneten nächsten Annäherung an die *Queen Elizabeth*. Das ARPA-System dient als Kollisionswarner und -vermeider ähnlich wie bei Flugzeugen. Obwohl die Radarsysteme 360 Grad Rundumsicht darstellen, steht während der einzelnen Wachen immer ein Ausguck mit Ferngläsern auf der Brücke, die nachts abgedunkelt wird, um die Sicht des Ausschau Haltenden nicht zu beeinträchtigen.

Ein Computersicherheitssystem zeigt den Wachhabenden auf Bildschirmen mit detaillierten Deckplänen jeden Winkel des Schiffes an. So können alle wasserdichten Türen, sämtliche Rauch- und Feuermelder – nicht nur in öffentlichen Räumen, sondern auch in jeder Kabine – Lüftung, Fahrstühle, Kühlanlagen und natürlich die Maschinen dargestellt, Probleme erkannt und über das System Maßnahmen eingeleitet werden.

The bridge is 36 metres wide and is located on deck 8, exceeding the ship's beam by two metres on both sides. From her wings, both sides of *Queen Elizabeth* are clearly visible, which is of immense help to the officers on the bridge as this offers an unobstructed view specially during the docking manoeuvres. For improving visibility further, large glass panels are inserted into the wing floors. The helmsman has free, unhampered vision directly downwards, which enables him to estimate the distance to the quay walls in an efficient manner. On both the bridge wings, there are consoles housing all the steering and computer elements. The same control panels are also in the wheelhouse, so that the ship can be manoeuvred from here too. At a bridge height of 26 metres, the horizon is approximately 18 kilometres away, but due to the bridge's height above the waterline; other ships even further away can be seen.

The bridge is equipped with state-of-the-art technical equipment, featuring large screens in the wheelhouse that display electronic nautical charts for the watch-keeping officers, the radar plottings, the collision warning and the safety system in varrious sizes and resolutions. This saves spaces – on *QE 2* approximately 1,800 nautical charts were held in stock, whereby today electronic charts based on the

charts of the British Admiralty are always up-to-date. The system is automatically updated every week, and receives corrections, i.e. new buoys or recently dredged fairways in the harbours. Additional printed nautical charts are also available for difficult passages. The chart table, where young officers can practise and gain further navigational knowledge, is located on the starboard side.

The present position is calculated by GPS (Global Positioning System). In addition to this, during every watch, an officer determines the ship's position by taking the position of the sun or the stars. He compares his calculated position with that indicated by the compass, in order to notice possible deviations, as the magnetic compass might be affected by the magnetic fields, caused by the ship's steel hull and the electronic devices. Radar scanners and processors assist to improve the safety at sea. The ARPA system (Automatic Radar Plotting Aid) is able to track up to 40 objects simultaneously and display them on the screens. Heading and speed of the tracked ships are displayed as well as the distance and the actual point in time when the ships get close to *Queen Elizabeth*. The ARPA system serves both as a collision warning and prevention system similar to that found in an aircraft. Although the radar systems display a 360 degrees panoramic view, there is always an officer on the look-out with binoculars during each watch. The light on the bridge is dimmed at night, in order to provide unimpaired visibility for the watch-keeper.

The watch-keeper uses a computerized safety system displayed on a screen, which provides detailed deck plans for every corner of the ship. All watertight doors, all smoke and fire alarm systems located not only in the public areas but also in every cabin, ventilation systems, elevators, cooling system and also the engines can be monitored on the screen. With this system, problems can be easily identified, and immediate and appropriate action can be taken.

DER MASCHINENKONTROLLRAUM
THE ENGINE CONTROL ROOM

Das Kontrollcenter befindet sich im Bauch des Schiffes in dem Crewbereich und ist nur für Befugte zugänglich. In dem vollklimatisierten Raum stehen wuchtige Computerpaneele, die u-förmig angeordnet sind. An der Decke hängen große Computer- und Fernsehbildschirme, die Aufnahmen von Überwachungskameras für die Motoren im Maschinenraum und einzelne Deckbereiche zeigen. Der Maschinenkontrollraum ist 24 Stunden am Tag und sieben Tage die Woche besetzt. Ein Zweiter Offizier, ein Dritter Offizier und ein sogenannter Motormann, der sich im Maschinenraum um die Motoren kümmert, sind pro Wache dabei. Die Wachhabenden befinden sich in ständigem Austausch mit der Brücke, von der Anweisungen zu Geschwindigkeit und Fahrtrichtung kommen. Insgesamt arbeiten hier 19 Ingenieure, Elektroingenieure und Elektroniker im Offiziersrang, dazu kommen noch 55 Techniker wie Schlosser, Mechaniker, Elektriker bis hin zum Klimaanlagenbauer.

Vom Kontrollcenter aus werden die Motoren, Generatoren und – sofern nicht gerade die Brücke ein Manöver fährt – auch die Antriebseinheiten überwacht und gesteu-

ert. Dazu kommen noch die Produktion von Frischwasser, die Klimaanlage sowie viele andere Aufgaben wie die Stromversorgung aller Kabinen und Funktionsräume. Von hier aus kann sofort reagiert werden, wenn ein Alarm ausbricht. In Sekundenschnelle wird der warnende Signalgeber lokalisiert, dann werden weitere Informationen zum betreffenden Vorfall gesammelt, ausgewertet und die notwendigen Maßnahmen eingeleitet, um das Problem blitzschnell zu lösen.

Selbst im Hafen läuft immer eine Maschine, damit die Küchen arbeiten können, das Licht angeht und die Klimaanlage läuft. Die Zeit im Hafen wird meist genutzt, um die Maschinen und Motoren zu überprüfen, einzustellen, zu warten oder bei Bedarf gar zu reparieren, die normalerweise in Betrieb sind, wenn die *Queen Elizabeth* sich auf See befindet. Große Reparaturen, zum Beispiel an den Pods, können aber nur im Trockendock vorgenommen werden.

The control centre is situated in the belly of the ship in the crew area. Only anthorised personal is allowed access

here. The computer panels in this fully air-conditioned room are arranged in all-shape. Large computer and TV screens hang down from the ceiling and display the recordings from the surveillance cameras in the engine room and certain deck areas. Lots of red, green and yellow knobs are on the panels and control desks, while instruments display the present cruising speed and the heading. The engine control room is occupied 24 hours a day and seven days a week. Every watch has one second officer, one third officer and one »engine man« who maintains the engines in the engine room. The watch-keepers are in permanent communication with the bridge, from where they receive instructions regarding speed and heading. There is a total of 19 engineers, both electrical and electronics. All are officers. They are assisted by around 55 technical staff: fitters, engineers, electricians and air-conditioning technicians.

The engines and generators as well as the propulsion units are monitored and operated from the control centre,

when the ship is not manoeuvred from the bridge directly. Further tasks include the production of fresh water, the air conditioning system as well as many other activities such as the power supply to all cabins and other areas. Immediate actions can be taken from here in the event of an alarm. The warning signal transmitter can be localised within seconds, followed by collection of further information in relation to the signalled alert. These information will be analysed further and the necessary actions will be implemented, to solve the problem immediately.

There is always one engine running in harbour, in order to keep the galleys operating, the lighting systems switched on and the air conditioning system running. The time in the harbour is mostly used to check, adjust and maintain the engines, or if necessary even to repair those, which are running when *Queen Elizabeth* is at sea. However, extensive repairs, for example to the pods, can only be carried out in a dry dock.

WILLKOMMEN AN BORD

WELCOME ABOARD

Die *Queen Elizabeth* ist nahezu ein Schwesterschiff der *Queen Victoria*. Wer einmal auf diesem Cunard-Liner gefahren ist, wird sich auch sofort auf der neuen Queen auskennen. Es gibt nur fünf Hauptunterschiede zur *Queen Victoria:* das Britannia Clubrestaurant ist nicht im Britannia Restaurant integriert; stattdessen steht den Gästen mit Kabinen in der höheren Britannia-Klasse jetzt ein eigenes Restaurant zur Verfügung. Dieses liegt auf Deck 2, zwischen dem Café Carinthia und dem Britannia Restaurant. Auf Deck 3 gibt es in Anlehnung an die *Queen Elizabeth 2* wieder eine Midships Bar. Der Wintergarten auf Deck 9 ist zu einer Garden Lounge geworden, aufgemacht wie ein großes Gewächshaus nach dem Vorbild der großartigen Glashäuser des Königlich Botanischen Gartens Kew Gardens in London. Auf Deck 11 sind im Sport- und Spielbereich ein Krocket und ein Bowling Green mit langen Kunstrasenflächen entstanden. Und der Grund für das etwas kastenförmig wirkende Heck sind 38 neue Kabinen, die dort eingebaut wurden. Mit einer maximalen Passagierkapazität von 2068 Reisenden kann die *Queen Elizabeth* 78 Gäste mehr aufnehmen als die *Queen Victoria*. Der größte Unterschied liegt aber in der Einrichtung, den Kunstwerken und der Ausstattung der öffentlichen Bereiche. Während die *Queen Victoria* ihrem Namen entsprechend gern als schwimmender viktorianischer Palast bezeichnet wird, ist die *Queen Elizabeth* ganz im Art déco-Stil der 1920er- und 1930er-Jahre eingerichtet. Insgesamt gibt es sechzehn Decks, zwölf davon sind für Passagiere zugänglich. Zur Ausschmückung wurden insgesamt 500 Kunstwerke im Wert von 2 Millionen Euro ausgesucht - Ölgemälde, Stiche, Drucke, Skulpturen, Intarsien, buntes Fensterglas und Fotografien - überwiegend von britischen Künstlern angefertigt. Die meisten Ölgemälde der

Queen Elizabeth is almost a sister ship to *Queen Victoria*. Whoever has travelled at least once on this Cunard liner, will in no time become familiar with the new Queen too. There are only five main differences w.r.t. *Queen Victoria:* the Britannia Club restaurant is not integrated in the Britannia restaurant. However, guests with cabins in the upper Britannia Class have an individual restaurant at their disposal on deck 2, located between the Café Carinthia and the Britannia restaurant. On deck 3, there is a Midships Bar, keeping in with the style of *Queen Elizabeth 2*. On this ship, the conservatory on deck 9 is named Garden Lounge, styled like a large conservatory resembling the magnificent glasshouses of the Royal Botanical Garden, Kew Gardens in London. The sport and games areas on deck 11 house croquet and a bowling green with long artificial turf alleys. The 38 new cabins, which were incorporated in this area, account for the slightly box-shaped appearance of the stern. The maximum passenger capacity of *Queen Elizabeth* is 2,068, 78 guests more than on *Queen Victoria*. However, the biggest difference can be found in the interior décor, the works of art and the furnishings of the public areas. According to her name, *Queen Victoria* was declared to be a floating Victorian palace, while *Queen Elizabeth* is completely furnished in the Art déco style of the 1920s and 1930s. In all there are sixteen decks, of which twelve are accessible to passengers. For decoration purposes, a total of 500 works of art (mainly from British artists) including oil paintings, engravings, prints, sculptures, inlays, coloured window glass and photographs, worth 2 million Euro, were selected. Most of the oil paintings of the Cunard ships such as the bulls eye paintings at the entrance of the Commodores Club were made by the young marine painter Robert Lloyd.

Die Ladenpassage wird durch die zwei-flügige Treppe dominiert und ist alten Londoner Einkaufsstraßen nachempfunden (vorhergehende Seite).

The shopping mall is dominated by a double-winged staircase and inspired by traditional London shopping arcades (previous page).

Kunstwerke für insgesamt mehr als zwei Millionen Euro wurden für das Schiff ausgesucht und zieren vor allem Treppenhäuser, Gänge und öffentliche Räume.

Works of art, in total worth more than two million Euros, were selected for the ship as decorations for the staircases, corridors and public areas.

Cunard-Schiffe, wie z. B. die Bullaugenbilder am Eingang vom Commodores Club, stammen von dem jungen Marinemaler Robert Lloyd. Kunstwerke, Fotos und Drucke schmücken nicht nur Bars, Restaurants und öffentliche Räume, sondern auch alle drei Treppenhäuser und die Kabinen.

Works of art, photos and prints decorate not only the bars, restaurants and public rooms, but also adorn the three staircases and the cabins.

HAUPTWANDBILD VOM NEFFEN DER QUEEN

MAIN WALL MARQUETRY PANEL BY THE QUEEN'S NEPHEW

Gäste betreten die *Queen Elizabeth,* je nachdem wie die Gangway im jeweiligen Hafen angelegt werden kann, auf Deck 1, der untersten Ebene der dreistöckigen Grand Lobby, oder eine Ebene höher auf Deck 2. Der erste Eindruck zählt, nach diesem Motto haben die Innenarchitekten diesen zentralen Punkt des Schiffes gestaltet.

Die verschwenderische Architektur und Ausstattung erinnern an das Design der großen Ozeanliner. Blickfang ist die große Freitreppe mit dem Geländer aus Gusseisen und einem Handlauf aus Mahagoni, die sich ein Stockwerk höher in zwei

Depending on the gangway position in each respective harbour, the guests enter *Queen Elizabeth* either on deck 1, at the lowest level of the three-tired Grand Lobby, or one level higher on deck 2. The interior designers have styled this central point of the ship, bearing in mind the importance of the motto: First impression is the best impression! The lavish architecture and furnishings remind one of the designs of the great ocean liners. An eye catcher is the big staircase with the balustrade made of cast iron and hand rails made of mahogany, which is divided into two sections one level higher. The curved glass balconies on three sides of deck 2 and 3 create a generous and lavish ambience for the Grand Lobby.

Das größte und auffälligste Kunstwerk hängt an der Stirnwand der Grand Lobby. Die 5,60 Meter hohe Reliefarbeit aus neun verschiedenen Edelhölzern zeigt die erste *Queen Elizabeth*.

The largest and most striking work of art hangs on the front wall of the Grand Lobby. The marquetry frieze, 5.60 metres high and made of nine different types of exotic wood, shows the first *Queen Elizabeth*.

Flügel teilt. Geschwungene Glasbalkone auf drei Seiten von Deck 2 und 3 lassen die Grand Lobby weitläufig und großzügig erscheinen.

Im Hintergrund der großen Freitreppe dominiert eine 5,60 Meter hohe Reliefarbeit aus Edelhölzern, die in einen überdimensionalen Torbogen eingebettet ist, als Blickfang die Grand Lobby. Das Kunstwerk erstreckt sich über zweieinhalb Decks und zeigt die Backbordseite des Bugs der ersten *Queen Elizabeth* von der Meeresoberfläche aus gesehen. Es besteht aus insgesamt neun Tafeln mit Intarsien, die nahtlos zu einer Platte zusammengefügt wurden. Neun verschiedene Holzarten sind als Furniere verarbeitet: pazifisches Madrona, indisches Ebenholz, amerikanischer Nussbaum, grauer Bergahorn, Esche, Vogelaugenahorn, Satinnussbaum, Wallnuss-

In the background of the wide staircase, a 5.60 metre high marquetsy panel of exotic woods, which is embedded in an oversized archway, dominates the Grand Lobby as an eye catcher. This work of art extends over two and half decks, featuring the portside of the bow of the first *Queen Elizabeth* as seen from the ocean surface. It consists of a total of nine panels with inlays, which are seamlessly joined to one wooden board. The veneers were made of nine different kinds of wood such as Pacific madrone, Indian ebony, American walnut, grey sycamore maple, ash, bird's eye maple, satin walnut, walnut burl wood and Macassar ebony. The order for this centrally located work of art in the heart of the ship went to the company of Viscount David Linley, the son of Princess Margaret and the Earl of Snowdon, who at the time of the order ranked

wurzelholz und Makassar-Ebenholz. Mit diesem zentralen Kunstwerk im Herzen des Schiffes wurde das Unternehmen von Viscount David Linley beauftragt, dem Sohn von Prinzessin Margaret und dem Earl of Snowdon, zum Zeitpunkt des Auftrags an dreizehnter Stelle der britischen Thronfolge: »Wir haben bereits viele Luxusyachten eingerichtet und verschönert, aber dieser Auftrag war etwas ganz Besonderes und das größte Bild, was wir bislang angefertigt haben.« Insgesamt dauerte es vier Tage, bis das gewaltige Kunstwerk im August 2010 auf der Fincantieri Werft an seinen Platz über der Treppe montiert war.

Rund um das intarsienverzierte Parkett im Mittelpunkt der Grand Lobby auf Deck 1 befinden sich die Rezeption, das Ausflugsbüro, ein ConeXXions Konferenzraum, das Internetcafé und vier Fahrstühle, die bis zu Deck 9 führen. Darin

thirteenth in the British line of succession: »We have already furnished and refurbished many luxury yachts, but this order was something very special and the largest panel we have made so far. « When the enormous work of art was mounted by Fincantieri shipyard in August 2010, it took a total of four days until it was finally fitted into its position place over the stairs.

The front desk, the excursion office, a ConeXXions conference room, the internet café and four elevators, which go up to deck 9, are located around the inlay decorated parquet flooring in the centre of the Grand Lobby on deck 1. The cabin numbers from 1001 to 1090 and the lower level of the Royal Court Theatre follow towards the bow, while the twelve cabins with add numbers 1089 to 1011 are situated on starboard towards the stern. The walk via the grand staircase, followed by taking the right wing upwards to deck 2, ends in the Verandah restaurant (sees chapter »Restaurants«, on page 102). The library entrance is located opposite the Verandah. This paradise for bookworms is designed in the style of old English libraries, two-storeyed with circular stairs, richly panelled with polished mahogany. The doors of the internally illuminated bookcases are made of ground glass. The dark wood, the glass doors and a lead glass dome, each of them with Tiffany inlays by John Hardman & Company, as well as the heavy reading chairs made of green leather create an ambience prevalent in England during the 19th century and entices the readers warmly. Two librarians look after approximately 6,000 books, and the collection of books is regularly reviewed and updated. The steps of the spiral stairs, when illuminated at night, reminds one of the classical circular corridor quintessential for English universities.

Die Wendeltreppe mit ihren beleuchteten Stufen fällt in der Bibliothek sofort ins Auge, das mindestens ebenso beeindruckende Oberlicht aus Tiffany-einlegearbeiten bemerken dagegen nur wenige Gäste sofort.

In the library the spiral staircase with its illuminated steps is a real eye-catcher. The skylight, which is just as impressive due to its Tiffany inlays, is not detected by many guest at first sight.

Die vergoldete Büste von Queen
Elizabeth II. am Eingang des Queens
Room stand ursprünglich auf der *QE 2*
(unten links).

The gold-plated bust of Queen
Elizabeth II at the entrance of the
Queens Room was originally on board
QE 2 (bottom, left).

Große Kronleuchter und das Holzparkett
bieten den Rahmen für ein festliches
Ambiente bei rauschenden Bällen
(unten rechts).

The grand chandeliers and the parquet
flooring provide the venue for a
gorgeous ball with a festive ambience
(bottom, right).

schließen sich zum Bug hin die Kabinen mit den Nummern 1001 bis 1090 und die untere Ebene des Royal Court Theaters an, Richtung Heck befinden sich steuerbord die zwölf ungeraden Kabinennummern 1089 bis 1011. Geht man die prächtige Freitreppe hinauf und nimmt den rechten Flügel hoch zu Deck 2, gelangt man zum Verandah Restaurant (siehe Kapitel Restaurants, S. 102). Gegenüber dem Verandah liegt der Eingang zur Bibliothek. Das Paradies für Leseratten ist im Stil alter englischer Bibliotheken gehalten, zweistöckig mit einer Wendeltreppe, reich mit poliertem Mahagoni vertäfelt. Die Bücherschränke sind von innen beleuchtet und werden durch Türen aus geschliffenem Glas geschützt. Das dunkle Holz, die Glastüren und eine Bleiglaskuppel, jeweils mit Tiffanyeinlegearbeiten von John Hardman & Company, sowie die schweren Lesesessel aus grünem Leder erzeugen ein Ambiente wie im England des 19. Jahrhunderts und laden zum Schmökern ein. Zwei Bibliothekarinnen wachen über rund 6000 Bücher, der Bestand wird regelmäßig ergänzt und aktualisiert. Die Wendeltreppe, deren Stufen abends beleuchtet werden, führt auf einen klassischen, umlaufenden Gang, wie man ihn von englischen Universitäten kennt.

The Café Carinthia is situated opposite to the library on deck 2 (see Bars and Cafés). Walking further towards the stern, passengers reach the Britannia Club restaurant and the lower level of the Britannia restaurant. On the way towards the bow, one encounters at first the museum trail, which is dedicated to the first *Queen Elizabeth* and *Queen Elizabeth 2*. On display within glass cabinets are exhibits shown for the first time such as logbooks, articles of daily use, model toys and many photos from the construction, the christening and from on board of both Queens.

QUEENS ROOM

The Queens Room is located aft of the museum trail. It is the ballroom of the ship. The 500 sqm two-storey salon, featuring approximately 250 sqm of hand-crafted parquet floor with inlays made of light maple wood, is dominated by two awesome crystal glass chandeliers. Many events take place here all day long, such as bingo, dancing classes or the captain's reception, the classic high tea in the afternoon as well as

Die Taufpatin, Englands Königin, ist
auch im hinteren Teil des Queens Room
stilvoll vertreten.

Her Majesty, Queen Elizabeth II, is also
stylishly represented in the aft section
of the Queens Room.

Gegenüber der Bibliothek befindet sich auf Deck 2 das Café Carinthia (siehe Bars und Cafés), geht man weiter Richtung Heck gelangt man zum Britannia Club Restaurant und der unteren Ebene des Britannia Restaurants. Richtung Bug stößt man zunächst auf den Museumspfad, der der ersten *Queen Elizabeth* und der *Queen Elizabeth 2* gewidmet ist. Interessierte finden hier erstmals gezeigte Ausstellungsstücke in Glasvitrinen, unter anderem Logbücher, Gebrauchsgegenstände, Spielzeugmodelle und viele Fotos von Bau, Taufe und von Bord der beiden Queens.

QUEENS ROOM

Hinter dem Museumspfad liegt mit dem Queens Room der Ballsaal des Schiffes. Der 500 m² große Salon, mit rund 250 m² großem, handgemachtem Parkettboden mit Intarsien aus hellem Ahornholz, ist zweistöckig und wird von zwei riesigen Kronleuchtern aus Kristallglas dominiert. Hier finden den ganzen Tag über Veranstaltungen wie Bingo, Tanzkurs oder Kapitänsempfang statt, der klassische High Tea am Nachmittag

balls and dance sessions in the evening. A total of 228 seats, located around the dance floor, are available at the lower level. Hanging balconies with curved hand rails offering a magnificent view of the dance floor are located on the port side of the hall. The balconies are on the upper circumferential level, under-pinned by marble columns. The starboard side is lighted with the help of large stained glass windows with Tiffany designs. The front wall is dominated by an orchestra stage, which can also be used for lectures and readings. The hall maintains the royal décor and traditions of the Cunard Line, like no other place on the ship. The walls feature paintings of royal palaces. The room above the dance floor is dominated by two magnificent chandeliers made of Swarovski crystals. The entrance hall exhibits a sculpture, which was on board the *QE 2* since 1969, but was excluded from the Dubai deal. From November 2008, it was stored away for later use on the new ship: a bust of Her Majesty Queen Elizabeth II, created by sculptor Oscar Nemon, is one of the most eye-catching and valuable pieces of art on board.

The famous English afternoon tea is a typical Cunard tradition, served here as high tea, celebrated by waiters

sowie Bälle und Tanzveranstaltungen am Abend. Insgesamt stehen 228 Sitzplätze auf der unteren Ebene zur Verfügung, die rund um das Parkett angebracht sind. Im oberen Umlauf, der von Marmorsäulen getragen wird, sind auf der Backbordseite zum Saal hin freitragende Balkone mit geschwungenen Handläufen und Blick auf das Tanzparkett angebracht, an der Steuerbordseite leuchten große Bleiglasfenster mit Tiffanyarbeiten. Die Stirnwand wird von einer Bühne eingenommen, auf der die Orchester spielen, aber auch Vorträge und Lesungen werden hier abgehalten. Über dem Tanzparkett dominieren zwei riesige Deckenleuchter aus Swarovski-Kristallen den Raum. Im Eingangsbereich steht eine Skulptur, die sich seit 1969 auf der *QE 2* befand, beim Dubai-Deal aber nicht mitverkauft, sondern ab November 2008 für die Verwendung auf dem neuen Schiff eingelagert wurde. Die vom Bildhauer Oscar Nemon geschaffene Büste der britischen Monarchin Queen Elizabeth II. gehört zu den auffälligsten und wertvollsten Kunstwerken an Bord.

Eine Cunard-Tradition ist der traditionelle englische Nachmittagstee, der hier als High Tea zelebriert und von Obern in weißer Livree und weißen Handschuhen serviert wird. Sand-

dressed in white livery and white gloves. They serve many variations of sandwich nibbles, delicious little pieces of cake and of course freshly baked scones with marmalade and clotted cream. A string quartet plays classical music in the background, creating a festive atmosphere that has become a trademark for the shipping company.

ROYAL ARCADES

Leaving the Queens Room through the aft exit, you will reach the Royal Arcades shopping mall, which is styled like a public square. The grandfather clock made by Dent & Co is the main attraction of the curved stairs at the end of the lower level of the two-storey shopping mall.

The shopping mall has more than 1,200 square metres of space, and on the lower level one can also gain access to the 500 sqm casino and the Golden Lion pub. It was designed with London shopping malls such as the Royal Arcades and the Burlington Arcades in mind; the same styling can be seen on *Queen Victoria* too. The large skylight provides for generous

Die Standuhr stammt vom ehrwürdigen Uhrmacherhaus und Hoflieferanten Dent & Co., die unter anderem auch die Uhr des Big Ben angefertigt haben (linke Seite).

The long case clock was made by the old-established clock maker firm and purveyor of the court Dent & Co., who have also manufactured the clock of Big Ben (left page).

Die Ladengalerie ist den Londoner Royal Arcades sowie den Burlington Arcades nachempfunden.

The design of the shopping mall is based on the Royal Arcade and the Burlington Arcade in London.

wich-Häppchen in vielen Variationen, köstliche Kuchenstückchen und natürlich frisch gebackene Scones mit Marmelade und Clotted Cream werden gereicht. Im Hintergrund spielt ein Streichquartett klassische Melodien, die diesem Brauch, der zu einem Markenzeichen der Reederei avancierte, einen beinah festlichen Hintergrund geben.

ROYAL ARCADES

Sobald man den Queens Room durch den hinteren Ausgang verlässt, gelangt man zur Royal Arcades genannten Einkaufszone, die wie ein öffentlicher Platz gestaltet ist. Hauptanziehungspunkt der geschwungenen Treppe am Ende der unteren Ebene der zweistöckigen Ladenpassage ist die von Dent & Co angefertigte Standuhr.

Die mehr als 1200 m² große Ladenpassage, von deren unteren Ebene auch das 500 m² große Spielcasino und der

light, and the circumferential walkway on the upper level of deck 3 allows for extensive window shopping like a boulevard on land.

Cunard Line invited Fortnum & Mason to open a shop on the gallery. It is the first time that this traditional English firm accepted to set up a business at sea. Established in 1707, Fortnum & Mason's, London-based department store on Piccadilly belongs to the exclusive circle of Royal Warrant Holders. On board, the range of goods includes tea blends, jams and preserves, finest pastries as well as gifts. The gentlemen's outfitter Hackett of London, a Harris Tweed store and the accessory designer Anya Hindmarch are other well-known British brands, who have set up a store on board a ship for the first time. Last but not least – and most important for all those who have forgotten their dinner jacket for formal evenings or even do not own one, have the chance the to hire from a comprehensive range of sizes for all occasions from Moss Bros Hire.

DER KÜCHENCHEF DER KÖNIGIN: NICHOLAS OLDROYD
THE HEADCHEF OF THE QUEEN: NICHOLAS OLDROYD

Der Küchenchef der *Queen Elizabeth* gebietet über eine Brigade von 80 Köchen und 65 Küchenhilfen aus aller Herren Länder, 11 000 Mahlzeiten kommen unter seiner Leitung auf den Tisch – jeden Tag. Da werden die Arbeitstage automatisch lang, meist fängt Nicholas Oldroyd morgens um sechs Uhr an und ist bis zum Mitternachtsbüfett auf den Beinen, nur nach dem Mittagessen hat er Freizeit. Wenn der Küchenchef nicht im Büro oder in Meetings sitzt, ist er ständig unterwegs und schaut sich in allen Restaurants die Präsentation und die Qualität der Speisen an.

Nicholas wurde in Bridlington, East Yorkshire, geboren und verbrachte seine Kindheit in North Yorkshire. Nach der Schule besuchte er das Scarborough Yorkshire Coast College, wo er ein Diplom in Catering & Hospitality erwarb. Bereits während seiner vierjährigen Studienzeit gewann er kulinarische Preise, so wurden ihm unter anderem der Titel »Chef of the Year« und der »St. Emilion Award« verliehen. Nach dem Studium ging Nicholas nach Frankreich und arbeitete in zwei Restaurants, die jeweils einen Michelin-Stern vorweisen konnten: dem Les Cedres in Darome und La Table De Frère Ibarboure in Biarritz. Nach seiner Rückkehr nach England wurde er Küchenchef des für sein hervorragendes Essen bekannten Cornucopia & Copper Horse Restaurant in North Yorkshire. Ein Jahr später tat er sich mit seinem Zwillingsbruder Mark zusammen, der ebenfalls eine Ausbildung zum Küchenchef gemacht hatte. Drei Jahre lang führten sie gemeinsam die Küche des North Yorkshire Golf Club in Strensell, York.

Im September 1999 entschieden sich die beiden Brüder, auf einem Schiff anzuheuern; sie wählten die *Queen Elizabeth 2*, weil einer ihrer Köche immer von seiner Zeit auf der *Queen Mary* geschwärmt hatte. Nicholas begann seine Cunard-Karriere als Demi Chef de Partie und arbeitete sich in sieben Jahren hoch bis zum Chef de Cuisine. Das Leben und Arbeiten an Bord übertraf seine Erwartungen: »Das Arbeiten ist völlig anders als an Land, an Bord muss man sich noch mehr auf sein Team verlassen. Es ist nicht so einfach in großen Mengen zu kochen und das so, dass es jedem Gast so schmeckt, als sei das Essen nur für ihn zubereitet worden. Und durch die Enge in den Küchen und die vielen Stunden, die man bei der Arbeit und auch hinterher im Crewbereich verbringt, entsteht schnell ein Familiengefühl, man kann seinen Leuten völlig vertrauen.«

Nach einem halben Jahr auf der *Queen Mary 2* gehörte Nicholas 2007 zur Startercrew der *Queen Victoria*. Im Mai 2008 wurde er Executive Sous Chef und somit zweiter Mann in der Küchenhierarchie, nur anderthalb Jahre später folgte die Ernennung zum Küchenchef und der Einsatz während der Jungfernsaison der *Queen Elizabeth*.

Wichtigstes Arbeitsgerät neben Probierbesteck und Kochlöffel ist der Computer. Am PC in seinem Büro erstellt er Menüpläne, plant die Speisenfolge für die nächsten Kreuzfahrten oder checkt den Bestand in den Kühlräumen. Bei der Zusammenstellung der täglichen Speisekarten und den daraus resultierenden Bestellungen muss der Küchenchef, der als Offizier drei Streifen trägt, die Vorlieben der Gäste richtig einschätzen: Transatlantik-Reisende, so seine Erfahrung, sind hungriger als Kreuzfahrt-Passagiere, und Deutsche ordern besonders gern Fisch, während Amerikaner Rindfleisch bevorzugen. Schalentiere gehen dagegen bei allen Nationalitäten gut, jede Woche bereitet die Küchencrew allein 400 Kilogramm Hummer zu.

Auch während seines Urlaubs sind Speisen die Berufung von Nicholas. Gemeinsam mit seinem Zwillingsbruder, der als Küchenchef auf der *Queen Victoria* arbeitet, hat er ein Haus in Kissimmee, Florida. Das größte Hobby der Brüder ist essen zu gehen und sich kulinarische Inspirationen zu holen. Nicholas liebt es, mit seinem Mercedes das Hinterland Floridas und neue Restaurants zu entdecken. Und auch das Wasser spielt im Urlaub eine Hauptrolle: Nach vier Arbeitsmonaten auf See entspannt sich Nicholas gern am eigenen Pool.

The chef of *Queen Elizabeth* is in charge of a brigade of 80 cooks and 65 kitchen assistants from all over the world. Under his command, no less than 11,000 meals are prepared every day. Consequently, his working days

are extremely long. Most of the times, Nicholas Oldroyd begins his work at six o'clock in the morning and he is busy until the midnight buffet has been served. His only leisure time is after lunch. When the chef is not in the office or in meetings, he is permanently on the go, inspecting the presentation and quality of meals at all the restaurants.

Nicholas was born in Bridlington, East Yorkshire and spent his childhood in North Yorkshire. After finishing school, he attended the Scarborough Yorkshire Coast College, where he obtained a diploma in catering and hospitality. Already during his four years of study, he won culinary awards such as »Chef of the Year« and the »St. Emillion Award«. After finishing his studies, Nicholas went to France and worked in two restaurants, both with one Michelin star each: the Les Cedres in Darome and La Table de Frère Ibarboure in Biarritz. Atter his return to England, he became chef of the Cornucopia & Copper Horse restaurant in North Yorkshire, renowned for its excellent meals. One year later, he started a joint business with his twin brother Mark, who had finished his training as a chef by that time. For three years, they were running the kitchen of the North Yorkshire Golf Club in Strensell, Yorkshire together.

In September 1999, the two brothers decided to work on a ship. They chose *Queen Elizabeth 2*, because one of their cooks had always been raving about his time on board *Queen Mary*. Nicholas began his Cunard career as demi chef de partie and got promoted within seven years to chef de cuisine. The life and work on board exceeded his expectations: »The work is completely different as on shore. On board, one must be able to rely on the team to an extent much greater than on land. It is not so easy to cook large quantities in such a way that every guest thinks that the meal was only prepared for him. The narrow galleys and the many hours, which are spent at work and afterwards in the crew area, soon create a sense of family, whereupon you can completely trust your people.«

After serving half a year on *Queen Mary 2*, Nicholas became a member of *Queen Victoria's* first crew in 2007. In May 2008, he was made executive sous chef and thus the second man in the kitchen hierarchy. Only one and a half years later he was appointed to chef, followed by an employment during the maiden season on board of *Queen Elizabeth*.

The most important tool next to the knife-case and cooking spoon is the computer in his office, where he

creates new meals, plans the menu for the next cruises or checks the stock in the cold stores. The chef, in officer's rank with three stripes on his uniform, has to keep an eye on the guests' preferences when he plans the daily menu cards and their orders: his experience is that Transatlantic travellers are hungrier than cruise passengers; Germans like fish, while Americans prefer beef. However, shellfish is a best-seller with all nationalities. Every week the kitchen crew is preparing 400 kilograms of lobster.

Even during his holidays, it is Nicholas' vocation to create meals. Together with his twin brother, who is chef on board *Queen Victoria,* he owns a house in Kissimmee, Florida. The brothers' greatest hobby is dining and thereby gaining culinary inspirations. Nicholas likes to drive around in his Mercedes and discover new restaurants in the Florida hinterland. During his vacations, water plays a major role: even after four months of working at sea, Nicholas prefers to relax in his own pool.

DIE KÜCHENLOGISTIK
THE KITCHEN LOGISTICS

Vom Early Bird Frühstück ab 6.00 Uhr bis hin zum Mitternachtsbüfett: Cunard Line verwöhnt die Gaumen der Gäste. An Bord erwartet die Reisenden ebenso eine Hommage an die Speisen der Cunard-Liner aus der goldenen Zeit der Kreuzfahrt wie moderne, internationale Kreationen: Es ist Teil des Konzepts, jede Mahlzeit zu einem Erlebnis werden zu lassen. Rund 25 Menükarten werden für jeden Tag auf See zusammengestellt. Etwa 11 000 Mahlzeiten werden täglich auf der *Queen Elizabeth* zubereitet, denn auch die rund 1000 Mann Besatzung muss verpflegt werden. Die notwendige Organisation und Vorbereitung spielt sich größtenteils in den für Passagiere nicht zugänglichen Bereichen ab; in den Lager- und Kühlräumen im Bauch des Schiffes sowie den vielen Vorbereitungsstationen für die Küchen.

Der Küchenchef hat hinter der Hauptküche des Britannia Restaurants sein Büro und leitet von hier aus eine Brigade von rund 80 Köchen und 65 Küchenhilfen aus aller Herren Länder. Jedes Restaurant hat seine eigene Küche mit eigenem Chefkoch und seiner Mannschaft. In der Hauptküche kümmern sich zehn Mitarbeiter in der kalten Küche um die Vorspeisen, im warmen Bereich sind 48 Mann im Einsatz, den Nachtisch stellen acht Pâtissiers her. Die anderen Küchenkräfte sind vor allem in der Vorbereitung im Einsatz, dabei werden nicht nur säckeweise Kartoffeln oder Gemüse geschnitten, es gibt eigene Fleisch-, Fisch-, Suppen- und Soßenküchen an Bord. Ein Bäcker- und ein Konditormeister mit jeweils mehreren Bäckern und Helfern stellen für alle Restaurants täglich Brotspezialitäten, Brötchen sowie Gebäck und Torten unter anderem für die traditionelle Tea Time her. Dazu kommen noch die Gemüseschnitzer, die zum Beispiel aus Tomaten kunstvolle Rosen zur Dekoration der Speisen zaubern. Wahre Künstler sind auch die Eisskulpteure, die mit einer kleinen Kettensäge mächtige Figuren für die Büffett herstellen. Für Sauberkeit sorgen insgesamt rund 90 Tellerwäscher und Reinigungskräfte mithilfe von gewaltigen Geschirrspülmaschinen; zwei Hygieneoffiziere wachen darüber, dass alle Qualitätsstandards in diesem Bereich eingehalten werden.

Cunard Line culinary masterpieces pamper their guests' palates, from the early bird breakfast served from 6 a. m. to the midnight buffet! On board, travellers expect not only an homage to the meals of the Cunard liners from the golden cruising era, but they are also eager to sample modern, international culinary delights: The Cunard management succeeds with its philosophy of »making every meal a unique experience«.

On *Queen Elizabeth,* approximately 11,000 meals are prepared every day; 1,000 men, officers and crew, have to be catered for too, and approximately 25 menu cards have to be issued every single day at sea. The necessary organisation and preparation mostly take place in those areas which are not accessible to passengers, such as the provision and cold stores inside the ship's belly as well as in the many preparation stations for the galleys.

The chef's office is located aft of the main galley of the Britannia restaurant. From here, he heads a brigade of approximately 80 cooks and 65 kitchen assistants from all over the world. Each restaurant has its own kitchen with an independent chef and a crew to assist him. In the main galley, ten assistants take care of appetizers in the cold dishes area, 48 men are busy in the hot dishes area, and the desserts are made by eight patissiers. The other kitchen assistants also participate in food preparing activities, such as peeling potatoes, cutting vegetables and meat. There are designated separate kitchens for meat, fish, soups and sauces on board. A baker and a pastry chef, both assisted by several bakers and helpers, are busy making daily specialities for all restaurants, rolls as well as pastry, gateaux and scones etc. for the traditional tea time. Furthermore, there are vegetable carvers, who create highly ornate decorations for making the dishes look even more appealing, such as beautiful roses made of tomatoes. The ice sculptors, who create giant sculptures for the buffets using a small chain saw, are also true artists. In total approximately 90 dishwashing staff and cleaners look after a clean and tidy kitchen, helped by massive dishwashers. Two health officers have to ensure compliance with all quality standards in this area.

1000 FLASCHEN WEIN UND CHAMPAGNER PRO TAG
1,000 BOTTLES OF WINE AND CHAMPAGNE PER DAY

Der Verbrauch der Küchen und Bars an Lebensmitteln sowie Getränken ist beeindruckend. An den Zahlen wird deutlich, welch gewaltige logistische Leistung erforderlich ist, damit es den Passagieren beim Essen an nichts mangelt. Pro Jahr werden in den Küchen der *Queen Elizabeth* verarbeitet:

The consumption of food and beverages in the galleys and bars is impressive. The numbers below give an indication of the enormous logistic demand and planning, which is necessary to satisfy all possible passenger demands as far as dining is concerned. The annual amount of products used in the galleys of *Queen Elizabeth* is as follows:

Eier	1 500 000	Stück		Eggs	1,500,000	each
Mehl	160 000	Kilo		Flour	160,000	kilos
Milch	600 000	Liter		Milk	600,000	litres
Kartoffeln	180 000	Kilo		Potatoes	180,000	kilos
Reis	200 000	Kilo		Rice	200,000	kilos
Gemüse	400 000	Kilo		Vegetables	400,000	kilos
Früchte	380 000	Kilo		Fruit	380,000	kilos
Rindfleisch	140 000	Kilo		Beef	140,000	kilos
Schweinefleisch	100 000	Kilo		Pork	100,000	kilos
Geflügel	87 000	Kilo		Poultry	87,000	kilos
Fisch	58 000	Kilo		Fish	58,000	kilos
Meeresfrüchte	34 000	Kilo		Seafood	34,000	kilos
Kaviar	750	Kilo		Caviar	750	kilos
Champagner / Sekt	125 000	Flaschen		Champagne / sparkling wine	125,000	bottles
Rotwein	125 000	Flaschen		Red wine	125,000	bottles
Weißwein	110 000	Flaschen		White wine	110,000	bottles
Bier	300 000	Flaschen		Beer	300,000	bottles
Fruchtsäfte	425 000	Liter		Fruit juice	425,000	litres
Tee	960 000	Beutel		Tea	960,000	bags
Kaffee	295 000	Liter		Coffee	295,000	litres

Die Gänge zum Parkett wurden mit historischen Theaterszenen verziert.

The murals along the corridors leading to the stalls feature historic theatre scenes.

Das dreistöckige Theater bietet 800 Zuschauern Plätze im Parkett und auf den Rängen, insgesamt 32 Gäste können in den 16 Logen Platz nehmen (rechte Seite).

The three-storey theatre offers seating for 800 spectators in the stalls and on the balconies. A total of 32 guests can be seated in the 16 boxes (right page).

Golden Lion Pub abgehen, ist wie auf der *Queen Victoria* nach dem Vorbild von Londoner Einkaufsmeilen wie den Royal Arcades und den Burlington Arcades gestaltet. Das große Oberlicht sorgt für großzügige Beleuchtung, den Umlauf der oberen Ebene auf Deck 3 kann man wie eine Flaniermeile zum ausgiebigen Schaufensterbummel nutzen. Für die Galerie konnte Cunard Line mit Fortnum & Mason erstmals eine englische Institution für ein Geschäft auf See gewinnen. 1707 gegründet und mit seinem Kaufhaus mitten Londoner Piccadilly gehört Fortnum & Mason zum erlesenen Kreis der Hoflieferanten. An Bord werden Teemischungen, Konfitüren und Eingemachtes, feinste Backwaren sowie Geschenkartikel angeboten. Mit dem Herrenausstatter Hackett of London, einem Harris Tweed Store und der Accessoire-Designerin Anya Hindmarch sind weitere bekannte britische Marken ebenfalls zum ersten Mal mit einem Geschäft auf einem Schiff. Ebenfalls dabei – und wichtig für alle, die ihren Smoking für formale Abende vergessen haben oder keinen besitzen, ist der Kleiderverleih: Moss Bros Hire bietet eine umfassende Auswahl in vielen Größen und für fast jede Gelegenheit.

ROYAL COURT THEATER

Hinter den Royal Arcades liegt das vordere Treppenhaus mit dem Eingang zum Royal Court Theater. Das dreistöckige Halbrund besteht aus Parkett und zwei Rängen und bietet 832 Plätze, davon 16 Balkonlogen für jeweils zwei Personen. Für 50 Dollar pro Paar pro Show kann man eine Loge über die Rezeption vorbestellen und wird dann von einem White Star Bell Boy mit weißen Handschuhen empfangen, der in einer Lounge Champagner und Desserthäppchen reicht. Zu Beginn der Vorstellung führt der persönliche Bell Boy die Gäste zu den Privatlogen und serviert Champagner sowie Schokolade. Nach der Vorstellung darf man mit diesem Arrangement hinter der Bühne die Schauspieler besuchen und bekommt so einen Einblick in Garderobe und Technik.

Das Ambiente gleicht denen der Theater im berühmten Londoner West End im 19. Jahrhundert. Der in Blau und Gold gehaltene Saal, die Samtsessel, in denen man fast versinken kann, und die verwendeten schweren Stoffe geben ein Gefühl von Exklusivität bei gleichzeitiger Gemütlichkeit. Auf der Bühne gibt es ein Novum bei Cunard Line: Für das neue Schiff wurde mit der Queen Elizabeth Theatre Company ein eigenes

ROYAL COURT THEATRE

The fore stairwell with the entrance to the Royal Court Theatre is situated aft of the Royal Arcades. The three-tier semicircle consists of stalls and two circles and offers 832 seats, among them 16 loges on balconies for two persons each. For 50 dollars per couple per show, a private box can be booked in advance at the front desk. A White Star bell boy wearing white gloves will welcome the guests, then he will serve champagne and appetizers in a lounge. Before the performance begins, the personal bell boy will usher the guests to their private boxes, serving them champagne and chocolate. The arrangement includes a visit backstage to see the actors' rooms and the stage technology after the performance.

The ambience is similar to London West End theatres in the 19th century. The regal blue and gold-coloured hall, the deep velvet armchairs, and the heavy fabrics create a feeling of exclusiveness and coziness at the same time. A novelty on this ship: Cunard Line founded the Queen Elizabeth Theatre Company, the ship's own ensemble with its own repertoire. A total of 29 singers, dancers, actors and musicians

Ensemble gegründet und ein eigenes Repertoire erarbeitet. Insgesamt 29 Sänger, Tänzer, Schauspieler und Musiker bieten viele neue musikalische Produktionen und gekürzte Fassungen beliebter Stücke. Darunter ist der Hit »Slice of Saturday Night«, ein beliebtes 1960er-Jahre-Nostalgiespektakel, erfolgreich in Großbritannien und den USA und die größte Show, die es bei Cunard je gab.

Außerdem werden Shakespeares »Wie es euch gefällt« und gekürzte Fassungen von Neil Simons Triple Bill mit »Last of the Red Hot Lovers«, »Plaza Suite« und »The Odd Couple« gezeigt. »Sing« bietet eine Musikshow mit Szenen aus zeitgenössischen Musicals, Pop und Evergreens, »La Danza« eine Tanzproduktion mit atemberaubender Choreografie. Das Royal Court Theater ist damit so gut wie jedes Londoner West End oder Broadwaytheater – sie bieten für jeden etwas.

Tagsüber finden im Theater Lesungen und Vorträge aus dem reichhaltigen Lektorenprogramm statt. Darüber hinaus wird auch auf der *Queen Elizabeth* Cunards preisgekröntes Programm »Insights« angeboten. Dies gibt Gästen die Möglichkeit, Vorträge, Workshops sowie Fragerunden von und mit Wissenschaftlern, Experten und Prominenten zu besuchen. Das Programm bringt Interessierte mit Persönlichkeiten aus den

offer many new musical productions and abridged versions of popular plays. Among them is the musical »Slice of Saturday Night«, a popular nostalgic pastiche from the 1960s, tremendously successful in Great Britain and USA. This is the largest show ever performed on a Cunard ship.

Furthermore, Shakespeare's »As You Like It« and abridged versions of Neil Simon's Triple Bill with »Last of the Red Hot Lovers«, »Plaza Suite« and »The Odd Couple« are also performed. »Sing« is a music show, staging scenes from contemporary musicals, pop and evergreen hits. »La Danza« is a dancing production with a breathtaking choreography. The Royal Court theatre is, as good as any London West End or Broadway theatre, offering enjoyment for everyone.

During the day, readings and lectures from the comprehensive lecturers' programme take place in the theatre. *Queen Elizabeth* also offers Cunard's award-winning programme »Insights«. This comprehensive programme gives the guests the opportunity to attend workshops and lectures, and speak to the scientist, experts and VIPs. The programme is intended as a get-together of interested guests and famous personalities from the fields of history, politics, world affairs, science, art and literature. It underlines

Das Logenkonzept mit dem persönlichen Bellboyservice wurde auf der *Queen Victoria* so gut angenommen, dass man es auch auf dem neuen Schiff übernommen hat.

The idea of having boxes with a personal bellboy service was accepted so well on board *Queen Victoria* that this concept is on the new ship too.

Bereichen Geschichte, Politik, Weltgeschehen, Wissenschaft, Kunst und Literatur zusammen. Es unterstreicht Cunards Haltung, dass Entertainment lohnende Erfahrung sein soll.

Auf Deck 3, der Höhe des zweiten Theaterranges, befinden sich vor allem die oberen Ebenen der mehrstöckig angelegten Räumlichkeiten wie Ladenpassage, Queens Room, Bibliothek, Grand Lobby und Britannia Restaurant. Im Wandelgang über dem Queens Room ist die Kunstgalerie untergebracht, wo zur Versteigerung stehende Werke gezeigt werden. Dahinter sind in der Cunard-Galerie die Fotoporträts berühmter Schauspieler, Sportler und Politiker aufgehängt, die in der Vergangenheit auf Cunard-Schiffen gereist sind. Gleich gegenüber auf der Backbordseite befindet sich das Konferenzzentrum ConeXXions. Auf der obersten Ebene der Grand Lobby befindet sich mit der Midships Bar ein Cunard-Klassiker – schon auf dem Vorgänger *Queen Elizabeth 2* war diese Bar viel besuchtes Herzstück der abendlichen Unterhaltung. Außerdem sind die Buchhandlung, ein ruhiger Raum für Karten- und andere Gesellschaftsspiele sowie die Galerie des Bordfotografen auf dieser Ebene untergebracht. Hier befinden sich auch die Zugänge zum ersten Außendeck: Auf diesem rundumlaufenden Promenadendeck können Passagiere zum ersten Mal frische Seeluft schnuppern.

KABINEN UND SUITEN

Die Decks 4 bis 8 sind ausschließlich Passagierkabinen vorbehalten. Die *Queen Elizabeth* verfügt über 1034 Kabinen in acht unterschiedlichen Oberkategorien, 20 Kabinen sind behindertengerecht ausgestattet. Es gibt lediglich 162 Innenkabinen und 146 eher kleine Außenkabinen mit Fenster.

Cunard's principle, that the entertainment on board should afford guests a provocative and rewarding experience.

On deck 3, being level with the second row of balconies of the theatre, are first of all the upper levels of the multi-tiered premises such as the shopping mall, Queens Room, Library, Grand Lobby and the Britannia restaurant. The art gallery, where works of art are displayed for auction, is accommodated in the area above the Queens Room. The Cunard gallery aft of it displays the photo portraits of famous actors, sportsmen and politicians, who have travelled on board of Cunard ships in the past. The conference centre ConeXXions is located right opposite on portside. The Midships Bar, a Cunard classic, is located on the top level of the Grand Lobby. This bar was already the highlight of night entertainment on board *Queen Elizabeth 2*. Furthermore, on this, there is the bookshop, a special room for card and other board games as well as the gallery of the ship's photographer. Access to the first exterior deck is possible here. On the circular promenade deck, the passengers are able to catch the sea breeze for the first time on board.

CABINS AND SUITES

The decks 4 to 8 are exclusively reserved for passenger cabins. *Queen Elizabeth* features more than 1,034 cabins in eight different top level categories, 20 cabins are accessible for the handicapped. There are only 162 inside cabins and 146 small outside cabins with windows. 85 percent of the cabins feature a balcony or a sun terrace, among them the 127 suites that belong to Grill class. The inside cabins measure 14 to 23 sqm, the outside cabins without balcony range from 17 to 19 sqm, the balcony cab-

Selbst die geräumige Schlafzimmer der Grand Suiten haben einen Balkonzugang (unten links und rechts).

The spacious bedrooms of the Grand Suites also have direct access to the balconies. (bottom, left/right)

Die Grand Suiten verfügen über einen eigenen Whirlpool (oben).

Each of the Grand Suites has its own Jacuzzi (top).

85 Prozent der Kabinen verfügen über einen Balkon oder eine Sonnenterrasse, darunter 127 Suiten der Grillklassen. Die Innenkabinen sind 14 bis 23 m² groß, die Außenkabinen ohne Balkon reichen von 17 bis 19 m², die Balkonkabinen beginnen bei einer Größe von 22 m² und sind bis zu 44 m² groß. Diese Kategorien speisen alle im Britannia Restaurant. Neu sind 39 Kabinen der Kategorie Britannia Club, die sich auf Deck 8 befinden und zwischen 24 und 44 m² groß sind; diese Gäste speisen im eigenen gleichnamigen Restaurant.

Für die Gäste der 61 Princess Grill Suiten mit 31 bis 48 m² ist ein Conciergeservice eingerichtet. Wohn- und Schlafbereich sind getrennt, das Bad ist mit einer Badewanne ausgestattet. Die Gäste speisen im Princess Grill, der Queens Grill ist für die Kategorien darüber reserviert. Dies sind zunächst die 35 Queens Grill Suiten mit einer Größe von 47 bis 72 m², die neben dem Conciergeservice auch rund um die Uhr bei Bedarf auf einen eigenen Butler zurückgreifen können. Neben einem großen Badezimmer sind diese Suiten mit einem eigenen Wohnbereich, einem großen Balkon sowie einer Bar mit Spirituosen, Weinen und alkoholfreien Getränken ausgestattet. Frische Blumenarrangements und Cocktailhäppchen am Abend werden ebenso kostenlos arrangiert. Die 25 Penthouses sind zwischen 48 und 66 m² groß und zusätzlich noch mit exquisiten Marmorbädern versehen.

Die Master Suiten und Grand Suiten sind auf der *Queen Elizabeth* nach berühmten ehemaligen Kommandanten der Cunard Line benannt. Die beiden Mastersuiten, nach Commodore Sir Ivan Thompson und Commodore Sir Edgar Britten benannt, liegen mittschiffs auf Deck 7 und sind 102 m² groß. Der geräumige Balkon, der etwa vier Mal so lang ist wie der einer Außenkabine, kann sowohl vom Schlaf- als auch vom Wohnbereich aus betreten werden und bietet ne-

ins from 22 sqm up to 44 sqm. All passengers of these categories dine in the Britannia restaurant. The size of the 39 cabins of the Britannia Club category, located on deck 8, ranges from 24 to 44 sqm. Their guests dine in a separate restaurant with the same name.

A concierge service is available for the guests of the 61 Princess Grill Suites, all of them from 31 to 48 sqm in size. The living room and bedroom are separate; the bathroom is also equipped with a bath tub. The guests dine in the Princess Grill, while the Queens Grill is reserved solely for the supreme categories. At the moment, there are the 35 Queens Grill Suites of 47 to 72 sqm

in size, offering a concierge service with an individual butler on call throughout the day and night. These suites feature a large bathroom, a separate living room, a large balcony as well as a bar filled with spirits, wine and soft drinks. Fresh flower arrangements and canapés in the evening are available free-of-charge too. The 25 penthouses measure from 48 to 66 sqm, and are equipped with exquisite marble bathrooms.

The master suites and grand suites on board of *Queen Elizabeth* are named after former famous commanders of the Cunard Line. The two master suites, each of them 102 sqm in size, named after Commodore Sir Ivan Thompson and Commodore Sir Edgar Britten, are situated midship on deck 7. The spacious balcony, approximately four times longer than the one on an outside cabin, can be accessed from the bedroom as well as the living area. It offers sun loungers and a dining area for a private dinner with friends.

The highest category has four Grand Suites, measuring between 128 and 139 sqm in size. The Commodore Sir James Charles and the Commodore Sir Cyril Illingworth Suites are situated at the stern of deck 6, both have a an expansive balcony which runs from the middle of the stern to the

Ruhige Abendstimmung an Deck, fast
alle Passagiere sind zum Dinner oder
im Theater (linke Seite unten).

Calm evening atmosphere on deck.
Almost all the passengers are dining or
in the theatre (left page, bottom).

ben Liegestühlen einen Essbereich für ein privates Dinner mit Freunden.

Die höchste Kategorie sind die vier Grand Suiten, die zwischen 128 und 139 m² groß sind. Commodore Sir James Charles- und Commodore Sir Cyril Illingworth-Suite liegen am Heck von Deck 6 und haben einen umlaufenden Balkon von der Mitte des Heckbereichs bis zur Seite des Schiffes. Hier gibt es nicht nur einen privaten Essbereich, sondern auch noch eine Open-Air-Bar. Die Suite hat einen großzügigen Eingangsbereich, ein Esszimmer für bis zu sechs Personen, einen Arbeitsbereich mit Büro, ein Schlafzimmer mit begehbarem Kleiderschrank und Blick durch Panoramafenster auf die See sowie ein geräumiges Wohnzimmer mit großem Flachbildschirm. Direkt darüber liegen ein Deck höher die Commodore Sir Arthur Rostron- und die Commodore Sir James Bisset-Suite.

AN DECK

Auf Deck 9 liegt das erste Sonnendeck, insgesamt gibt es auf der *Queen Elizabeth* mehr als 3400 m² Platz zum Bräunen. Als erstes fällt langjährigen Cunard-Gästen der Bodenbelag auf: Anstatt der gewohnten durchgängigen Teakdecks wie auf *Queen Elizabeth 2* und *Queen Mary 2* sind die Außendecks auf der *Queen Elizabeth* mit einem pflegeleichten Gummibelag ausgestattet, auf dem das für Holzdecks typische Linienmuster aufgedruckt ist. Grund für diesen für Cunard Line ungewöhnlichen Belag sind die ab 2010 geltenden internationalen Feuerverhütungsvorschriften auf See, die nur noch einen bestimmten Prozentsatz an Echtholz auf Schiffen erlauben – und dieses Kontingent war durch die luxuriöse Gestaltung der Innenräume bereits verbraucht.

Das 1280 m² große Sonnendeck befindet sich am Heck und verfügt über einen 10 x 3 Meter großen Pool mit zwei separaten Whirlpools. Die Lido Pool Bar sorgt für erfrischende Getränke, genau gegenüber an Backbord ist der Lido Pool Grill, der Hamburger und andere Snacks bereithält. Auf einer kleinen Bühne in der Mitte lassen karibische Bands fröhliche Rhythmen erklingen. Gleich nach dem Sonnendeck kommt man auf dem Weg zum Bug in das Lido Büfettrestaurant, das sich über 1100 m² erstreckt, 468 Plätze bietet und den größten Teil von Deck 9 einnimmt. An das Lido Restaurant schließt die völlig neu konzipierte Garden Lounge an, die mit ihrer großflächigen Verglasung sowohl auf die See als auch in

ship' side. Here in addition to a private dining area, an open air bar is also installed. The suite has a generously dimensioned entrance hall, a dining room for up to six persons, an office and a bedroom with walk-in wardrobe. It has magnificent sea views through the panoramic windows as well as a spacious saloon with a large flat screen TV. The Commodore Sir Arthur Rostron and the Commodore Sir James Bisset Suites are located one deck higher directly above.

ON DECK

On board *Queen Elizabeth,* the first sun deck is located on deck 9, offering a total area of more than 3,400 sqm for sun bathing. The flooring on *Queen Elizabeth* immediately attracts the attention of Cunard guests, who are familiar with the other Cunard ships. Instead of the usual teak decks such as the ones on *Queen Elizabeth 2* and *Queen Mary 2* these outside decks on board *Queen Elizabeth* have a low-maintenance rubber coating, with the typical linear pattern of wooden decks printed on it. The reason for this unusual floor material on board a ship of the Cunard Line is the international fire protection regulations at sea, coming into effect from 2010, which only permit the usage of a certain percentage of natural wood on ships. This quota was already used up by the luxurious styling of the interior furnishings.

The 1,280 sqm sun deck is located at the stern, featuring a 10 x 3 metre pool with two separate Jacuzzis. The Lido Pool Bar offers refreshing beverages. Directly opposite on portside Hamburgers and other snacks are available in the Lido Pool Grill. Caribbean bands play cheerful songs on a small stage in the centre. Towards the bow, after leaving the sun deck, one arrives at the Lido buffet restaurant, which extends over an area of 1,100 sqm, offering 468 seats. It occupies the largest part of deck 9. The Lido restaurant is followed by the Garden Lounge, a design with a new concept. Its large glass windows allow for excellent seaviews and the skyviews, providing a mesmerizing feeling and appreciation of infinity. The outside Midships or Pavilion pool can be accessed through glass doors. The raised glass coaming is an excellent wind protection. For this reason the pool is highly frequented during days at sea. At the back of the pool, stairs lead to a raised wooden platform with two flush-mounted Jacuzzis.

den Himmel blicken lässt und so ein Gefühl von endloser Weite gibt. Geht man durch die Glastüren nach draußen, gelangt man zum Midships oder Pavillon Pool, der durch die hochgezogenen, verglasten Bordwände besonders windgeschützt und dadurch gerade an Seetagen sehr beliebt ist. Gleich hinter dem Pool führen Treppen auf eine Ebene aus Holz, in die zwei Whirlpools eingelassen sind. Backbord an der Stirnseite kann man sich an der Pavillon Pool Bar köstliche Cocktails mixen lassen. Durch die anschließenden Türen gelangt man in den SPA-Bereich.

SPA- UND FITNESSCENTER

Besonders großen Wert hat Cunard Line auf die Gestaltung des Spa- und Fitnessbereichs gelegt. Das Herzstück der 1200 m² großen Wohlfühlfläche bildet das sogenannte Royal Bathhouse, das einen großen Innenpool mit Hydrodüsen, eine weitläufige Saunalandschaft und Ruheräume umfasst. Die im SPA angebotenen Behandlungen sind von ostasiatischen, arabischen und orientalischen Einflüssen sowie dem Ayurvedaprinzip geprägt, eine Spezialität sind die indischen Massagen mit Kräutern und Ölen. Außerdem stehen sechs unterschiedliche Akupunktur-Behandlungen zur Auswahl.

Dieser Bereich ist teilweise auf zwei Ebenen angelegt, so befindet sich das Rasulbad eine Etage höher auf Deck 10.

At the front side on port, the Pavilion Pool Bar offers delicious cocktails. The spa area can be accessed through adjoining doors.

SPA AND FITNESS CENTRE

Cunard Line has attached great importance to the styling of the spa and gym areas. The so-called Royal Bathhouse forms the core of the 1,200 sqm wellness area, which includes a large indoor pool with water jets, a spacious sauna area and rest rooms. The treatments offered in the spa are characterised by East-Asian, Arabic and oriental influences as well as the Ayurveda principle. The Indian massages with herbs and oils are also very special and unique. Furthermore, guests have the choice of six different acupuncture treatments.

This area is partly located on two levels. The Rhassoul bath is situated one level higher on deck 10. Furthermore, products of the British noble brand Elemis are also available aboard the ship. In this area there is also a hair dresser and a nail studio offering various treatments and St. Tropez Sunless Tanning. The large gym has state-of-the-art exercise machines and a fantastic ocean view through the extreme oversized windows. There is another area were classes, that have to paid, for take place: aerobics, stretching, Thai yoga and meditation.

Auch im Ruhebereich des SPA genießt man den Blick auf den endlosen Ozean (linke Seite).

Guests have unlimited sea views from the rest area in the SPA (left page).

Erstmals betreibt Cunard Line das SPA mit verschiedenen Partnern in Eigenregie (unten).

For the first time, Cunard Line runs the SPA independently, assisted by some partner companies.

Ein Friseur, ein Nagelstudio sowie ein Solarium von St. Tropez Sunless Tanning runden das Angebot ab. Der große Fitnessbereich bietet neben modernsten Ausdauer- und Kraftgeräten einen tollen Meerblick aus übermannshohen Fenstern. Für Kurse wurde ein eigener Bereich geschaffen, in dem kostenpflichtiger Unterricht wie Aerobic und Stretching oder Thai-Yoga und Meditationsprogramme stattfinden.

Am auffälligsten auf Deck 10 ist das Dreiviertelrund des Yacht Clubs mit seinen halbrunden, mannshohen Fenstern, die einen 270 Grad weiten Rundblick über den Midships Pool und die See bieten. Geht man Richtung Bug, stößt man auf ein weiteres originales Stück der Queen Elizabeth 2: die Schiffsglocke. Sie wurde direkt in den Eingangsbereich des Gangs aufgehängt. Weiter vorn befindet sich die Zigarrenlounge Churchills, die unmittelbar daran anschließende Admirals Lounge kann für private Feiern reserviert werden und wird ansonsten für Kurse, Vorträge oder Gesellschafts- und Kartenspiele sowie für Bridge-Turniere genutzt. An der Vorderfront schließlich liegt der Commodore Club, aus dessen Panoramafenstern man tagsüber die gleiche Aussicht genießt wie die wachhabenden Offiziere auf der Brücke.

Ebenfalls auf Deck 10 befindet sich beim mittleren Treppenhaus die von SMC Design entworfene Spielzone für Kinder mit zwei Innen- und Außenspielplätzen. In den beiden voneinander getrennten Zonen backbord und steuerbord können Kinder nach Altersgruppen eingeteilt nach Herzenslust toben und Lärm machen, ohne Passagiere zu stören, die sich in Ruhe sonnen möchten. Wer dagegen an Deck Sport treiben will, findet unter der Treppe, die nach oben zum abgeteilten Deck für die Passagiere der Grillklassen führt, einen Golfabschlagsplatz und eine Tischtennisplatte.

Die Treppe hinauf gelangt man zu dem Areal mittschiffs auf Deck 11, das für die Gäste der oberen Kategorien reserviert ist. Hier befinden sich die beiden Restaurants Princess Grill und Queens Grill. An die Restaurants schließt sich die Grill Lounge an, in der sich der Concierge Service für die Passagiere der Suiten befindet und Nachmittagstee, Snacks und Cocktails serviert werden. Zwischen den beiden Restaurants ist, nach dem großen Erfolg auf der Queen Victoria, wieder der sogenannte Court Yard für Queens und Princess Grill-Gäste geschaffen worden; er bietet die Möglichkeit, unter freiem Himmel zu speisen. Vor den Restaurants stehen Liegestühle auf der Grills Terrace, dem exklusiven Sonnendeck, das über eine Treppe mit der Upper Grills Terrace, dem Sonnenbereich

The thee-quarter circle of the Yacht Club with its semicircular, six feet windows, offering 270 degrees of panoramic views over the Midships Pool and the sea, is the most distinctive and prominent feature on deck 10. Walking towards the bow, one finds another original part from Queen Elizabeth 2, which was also not sold in the Dubai contract: The ship's bell of QE 2 hangs right at the entrance of the corridor. Churchill's Cigar Lounge is located further forward, directly followed by the Admirals Lounge, which can be booked for private parties, when it is not used for courses, lectures or board and card games as well as for bridge tournaments. The Commodore Club with its panoramic windows, from where one can enjoy the same views throughout the day as the watch-keeping officers on the bridge, is situated at the front section.

The play area for children with two indoor and outdoor playgrounds, created by SMC Design, is also located on deck 10 near the central staircase. In two separate zones, one on port and one on starboard, children in different age groups can play and make noise to their heart's content – without any fear of disturbing passengers enjoying a sunbath. Those passengers that are interested to exercise on deck, will find a

DIE WÄSCHEREI
THE LAUNDRY

In der Wäscherei tief unter Deck ist es stickig und sehr warm, obwohl permanent die Klimaanlage läuft. Ein Teil der Reinigungskräfte sortiert Berge von Schmutzwäsche, die dann in die riesigen Trommeln der Industriewaschmaschinen wandern. Bis zu 100 Kilogramm nimmt jede der sechs Maschinen auf, gegenüber laufen große Trockner auf Hochtouren. Jeden Tag werden hier allein für die Gäste 7500 Handtücher, 6000 Badelaken, 10 000 Waschlappen und 3000 Badematten gewaschen, getrocknet, gebügelt und gefaltet. Dazu kommen noch einmal 4000 Poolhandtücher und 7000 Servietten.

Früher arbeiteten in den Wäschereien an Bord fast ausschließlich Chinesen, heute sind hier auch viele Indonesier und Philippiner beschäftigt. Insgesamt 32 Mann kümmern sich im Schichtdienst nicht nur um die Wäsche für den Hotelbetrieb – alle drei Tage kommen zu der normalen Tagesmenge Handtücher und Servietten noch 1100 Bettbezüge, 1100 Bettlaken und 6000 Kissenbezüge hinzu –, sondern auch um die von den Gästen zur Reinigung gegebenen Hemden, Hosen und Kleider. Diese werden ebenso mit speziellen Maschinen gewaschen oder trocken gereinigt wie die Uniformen und die Dienstkleidung der Crew. Während

die Hemden mit der Hand gebügelt werden, ziehen große Mangelmaschinen Bettwäsche und Handtücher nicht nur glatt, sondern falten sie in einem zweiten Schritt auch noch zusammen. Außerdem haben hier unten auch zwei Schneider ihren Arbeitsplatz, die lose Uniformnähte zusammenfügen, kleine Risse reparieren oder lose Knöpfe annähen.

Although the air conditioning system is running, the air in the laundry deep down below the decks is muggy and very warm. Some cleaners busily sort masses of laundry and load them into the huge drums of the washing machines. Each of the six machines has a capacity of up to 100 kilograms. The large tumble dryers usually run at full speed. Every day, 7,500 towels, 6,000 bath towels, 10,000 flannels and 3,000 bath mats are washed, dried, ironed and folded, plus 4,000 pool towels and 7,000 napkins.

In earlier times, there were mostly Chinese people working in the laundries on board. But today there are also many Indonesian and Filipino shift workers, totalling to 32 men. In addition to the normal daily quantity of towels and napkins for the hotel, 1,100 duvet covers, 1,100 bed sheets and 6,000 pillowcases have to be washed every third day, Shirts, trousers and dresses from the guests are cleaned too. These are washed or dry-cleaned using special equipment. The uniforms and working clothes of the crew are handled in the same way. While the shirts are ironed by hand, bed linen and towels are passed through large ironing machines, and are folded after that. Furthermore, two tailors take care of repairing uniforms i. e. mend uniform stitches, repair small tears or sow on loose buttons.

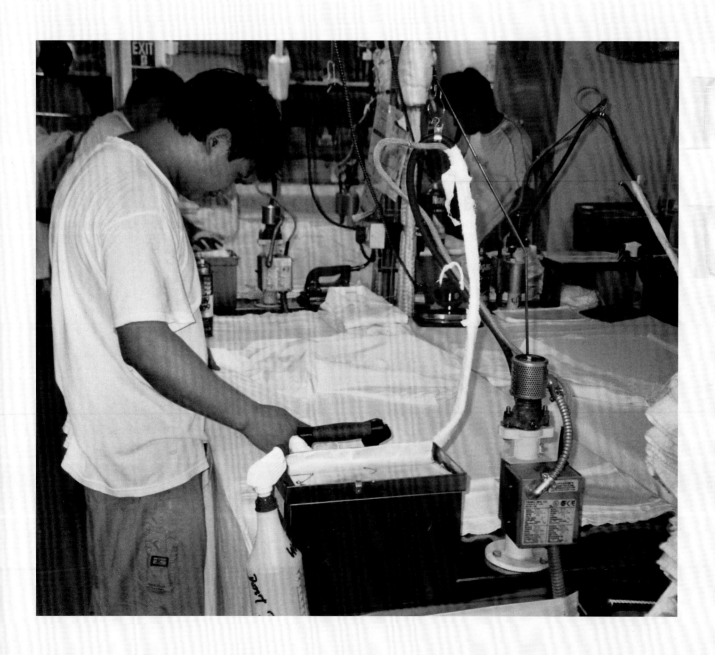

Das Royal Bathhouse ist das Herzstück des SPA (vorhergehende Doppelseite).

The Royal Bathhouse forms the heart of the SPA (previous double-page).

Zusätzliche Motivation: Auf den modernen Laufbändern hat man eine fantastische Aussicht.

Extra motivation: running on the modern treadmills offers fantastic views.

driving range and a ping pong table below the stairs, which lead upwards to a separate deck for the passengers of the Grill classes.

The area midships on deck 11, accessible via the upward stairs, is reserved for the guests of the upper categories. Here are the two restaurants Princess Grill and Queens Grill, followed by the Grill Lounge. This lounge, where tea, snacks and cocktails are served in the afternoon, accommodates also the concierge service for the suite passengers. Being a great success on *Queen Victoria,* a similar »Court Yard« for the Queens and Princess Grill guests was established between the two restaurants. This permitts the guests to dine alfresco. On the Grills Terrace in front of the restaurants sun loungers are provided. This exclusive sun deck is connected to the Upper Grills Terrace, the sunbathing area on deck 12, by a staircase. A raised platform can be used as lookout and is very popular when the ship leaves a harbour.

As on *Queen Victoria,* the sport deck is located in the front fore bow area on deck 11. However, the styling and the sport facilities are different. In addition to a basketball court, putting green and a playing field for paddle tennis, a bowling green and a croquet green were built for the first time on a Cunard ship. Here, the games are played on artificial turf. The two bowling lanes are installed transverse to the direction of travel. When playing, the large windows permit a fantastic view of the horizon.

auf Deck 12, verbunden ist. Hier befindet sich auch eine erhöhte Plattform als Ausguck, die vor allem beim Auslaufen aus Häfen genutzt wird.

Das Sportdeck ist wie auf der *Queen Victoria* Richtung Bug ganz vorn auf Deck 11, neu sind aber die Gestaltung und die Spielmöglichkeiten. Denn neben Basketballplatz, Putting Green und einem Spielfeld für Paddle Tennis wurden erstmals auf einem Cunard-Schiff ein Bowling Green und ein Krocket Green angelegt. Auf Kunstrasen können hier die Partien gespielt werden, die beiden Bowlingbahnen liegen quer zur Fahrtrichtung, durch die großen Fenster hat man beim Spielen einen tollen Blick auf den Horizont.

STILVOLL SPEISEN –
DIE RESTAURANTS AN BORD

Selbstverständlich bietet die *Queen Elizabeth* zahlreiche Möglichkeiten zu dinieren. Ob stilecht in einem der vier Hauptrestaurants, leger in einem der Themenrestaurants des Lido Buffet Restaurants oder raffiniert zubereitet im Verandah Restaurant. Die umfangreiche Weinkarte trägt dazu bei, dass jede Mahlzeit zu einem einmaligen Ereignis wird. Die Reisenden erwartet eine liebevolle Hommage an die alten Restaurants an Bord der früheren Cunard-Liner ebenso wie moderne, internationale Küchenkonzepte. Die Reederei Cunard Line verwöhnt aber nicht nur die Gaumen ihrer Gäste, sondern wartet zudem mit dem exzellenten White Star Service auf. Der Cunard-Tradition entsprechend entscheiden Gäste mit der Buchung ihrer Unterkunft, in welchem der vier

STYLISH DINING –
RESTAURANTS ON BOARD

Queen Elizabeth offers numerous dining options. Guests may dine in elegant style in one of the four main restaurants, visit one of the theme-restaurants of Lido Buffet for a casual meal or savous the exquisite and contemporary French cuisine in the Verandah restaurant. For this new restaurant, Cunard Line's top chef, Jean-Marie Zimmermann, created special recipes. The comprehensive wine list makes every meal a unique experience. The travellers on *Queen Elizabeth* may expect a loving homage to the old restaurants on board of the former Cunard liners as well as modern international cuisine. Cunard Line does not merely spoil the palates of their guests; but still offers them their excellent White Star Service. In line with Cunard's tradition,

Der kulinarische Botschafter von Cunard Line, Jean-Marie Zimmermann, hat alle Gerichte des Gourmetrestaurants selbst kreiert.

Jean-Marie Zimmermann, Cunard Line's Global Culinary Ambassador, has personally created all the dishes for the gourmet restaurants.

Hauptrestaurants sie speisen. Zur Auswahl stehen das herrschaftliche Britannia Restaurant, das intime Britannia Club Restaurant, das exklusive Princess Grill Restaurant oder das luxuriöse Queens Grill Restaurant. Bis auf das Lido sind alle Restaurants mit vielen Art déco-Elementen und reichhaltigen Holzvertäfelungen ausgestattet. Mosaike, Skulpturen und Bilder sowie herrschaftliche Deckenleuchter und die großzügige Verwendung von Marmor sind darauf abgestimmt, die Optik der Speisesäle der großen Ozeanliner mit elegantem Dekor widerzuspiegeln, so Cunard-Präsident Peter Shanks: »Bei der Planung für diese Restaurants haben wir uns von den Entwürfen inspirieren lassen, die Cunard Line im Laufe der Geschichte geschaffen hat und die Highlights hieraus weiterentwickelt. Es war uns wichtig, unsere glanzvolle Vergangenheit mit innovativen Neuerungen zu kombinieren, die auf die Bedürfnisse der anspruchsvollen Gäste von heute ausgerichtet sind.«

the guests can opt at the time of cabin-booking, in which of the four main restaurants they would prefer to dine. They can choose from the grand Britannia restaurant, the intimate Britannia Club restaurant, the exclusive Princess Grill restaurant or the luxurious Queens Grill restaurant. Except the Lido, all the restaurants are furnished with many Art déco elements and rich wood panellings. Mosaics, sculptures and paintings as well as grand chandeliers and the magnanimous usage of marble were harmoniously matched in order to reflect the visual effects of the elegantly styled dining-halls of the big ocean liners. Cunard president Peter Shanks said: »With the debut of *Queen Elizabeth*, Cunard will become one of the oldest names in Ocean travel, sailing the industry's youngest fleet, so it is natural for us to recognize our past while always innovating for the future needs of our discerning traveller.«

VERANDAH GRILLS

Die Verandah Grills auf der *Queen Mary* und der *Queen Elizabeth* galten als die exklusivsten Speisesäle auf See, die den damals vornehmsten, privaten Clubs in London, New York und Paris

VERANDAH GRILLS

The Verandah Grills on board *Queen Mary* and the original *Queen Elizabeth* were classified as the most exclusive dining rooms at sea, on a par with exlusive private clubs in London, New York and Paris at that time. On the former

Im Restaurant Verandah schaffen
helle Farben und edle Materialien
ein Wohlfühl-Ambiente.

Light colours and fine materials in
the Verandah Restaurant make you
feel good.

in nichts nachstanden. Auf den ersten Queens standen die Verandah Grills den Passagieren der Ersten Klasse zur Verfügung, hier waren die königliche Familie, Filmstars sowie die Reichen und Schönen zu Gast. Im Verandah Grill, der sich auf Deck 2 befindet und 104 Plätze bietet, gibt es feinste französische Küche. Jean-Marie Zimmermann, langjähriger Küchenchef auf Cunard-Schiffen und jetzt als »kulinarischer Botschafter« für die Entwicklung neuer Speisen, das Qualitätsmanagement der Küchen und die Menüpläne an Bord aller drei Queens zuständig, hat eigens Gerichte kreiert, die er als Hommage an seine Heimat sieht. Die Gerichte nehmen die Gäste mit auf eine kulinarische Reise durch Frankreich und bringen ihnen die Besonderheiten und den Geschmack von Regionen wie Périgord, den Pyrenäen, Elsass, Burgund und Bresse nahe. Hochwertige Produkte bester Herkunft werden mit höchster Kochkunst kombiniert, um ein ultimatives Geschmackserlebnis zu gewährleisten. Gourmets können sich auf kulinarische Meisterwerke wie zum Beispiel Seeteufel und Bouillabaisse, Magret Ente, gebackenen Brie de Meaux Brioche und mit Edmond Briottet Crème de Peche gefülltes, heißes Vanille Soufflé freuen.

Der helle und elegant eingerichtete Raum bietet den perfekten Rahmen für ein kulinarisches Erlebnis der Extraklasse. Die Gemälde des Restaurants sind angelehnt an die Wandmalereien an Bord der ersten beiden Queens. Das kulinarische Erlebnis wird abgerundet von hochwertigen Gedecken mit feinstem Wedgwood Porzellan, Waterford Kristallgläsern, Tafelsilber von Gainsborough und Bestecken von Hepp. The Verandah ist mittags von 12.30 bis 14 Uhr und abends von 18.30 bis 21.00 Uhr geöffnet und steht allen Gästen zur Verfügung. Die hier angebotenen Mahlzeiten sind kostenpflichtig.

BRITANNIA RESTAURANT

Die elegante Doppeltreppe des zweistöckigen Hauptrestaurants bietet die perfekte Bühne für einen Gala-Auftritt. Gäste speisen im geschmackvollen Art déco-Ambiente wahlweise in der frühen Sitzung ab 18.00 Uhr oder in der späten Sitzung ab 20.30 Uhr. Zum Frühstück und Mittagessen herrscht hier bei einer offenen Sitzung freie Platzwahl. Das Britannia Restaurant befindet sich auf den Decks 2 und 3 und bietet insgesamt 878 Sitzplätze. 512 Plätze befinden sich auf der 1087 m² großen unteren Ebene, 366 Plätze auf 750 m² eine Etage höher.

Queens, the Verandah Grills were exclusively available to First Class passengers, as well as to the Royal Family, film stars and the rich and famous. In the Verandah Grill, located on deck 2, offering 104 seats, finest French cuisine is served. Jean-Marie Zimmermann, who was also chef on board of other Cunard ships, being a »Global Culinary Ambassador« is responsible for the creation of new meals, the quality management of the galleys and or the menus on board of all three Queens. He has created special meals paying homage to his homeland. The dishes served will take guests on a culinary journey through France, evoking the special personality and flavour of regions such as Périgord, the Pyrenees, Alsace, Burgundy and Bresse. First-class products from the first purveyors are combined with the best methods to achieve the quintessential taste experience. Gourmets can enjoy culinary masterpieces such as Monkfish and Bouillabaisse, Magret Duck, Baked Brie de Meaux Brioche and Hot Vanilla Soufflé, infused with Edmond Briottet Peach Liquer.

The bright and elegantly styled rooms offer the perfect ambience for a culinary experience in a class of its own. The paintings of the restaurants follow the model of the mural paintings on board of the early Queens. The culinary experience is enhanced by top quality table decorations: finest Wedgwood china, Waterford crystal glasses, silverware by Gainsborough and cutlery by Hepp. At lunchtime, the Verandah is open from 12.30 to 2 p. m. and in the evenings from 6.30 to 9 p. m. It is open to all guests. The meals offered here are charged separately.

BRITANNIA RESTAURANT

The elegant twin stairs of the two-tiered main restaurant offer the perfect stage for a brilliant performance. The guests dine in the elegant Art déco ambience, either at the early sitting starting 6 p. m. or in the late setting from 8.30 p. m. onwards. Breakfast and lunch are served by open seating. The Britannia restaurant, situated on deck 2 and 3, offers a total of 878 seats. 512 seats are placed on the 1,087 sqm lower level, 366 seats one level higher on 750 sqm. As the restaurant is located at the stern, large panoramic windows allow a spectacular view of the sea during the meal. A three metre high Art déco mural

Die elegante Doppeltreppe sorgt für das richtige Entrée in das Britannia Restaurant.

The elegant twin stairs give an extraordinary access into the Britannia restaurant.

Ein Teil des Lido Buffet Restaurants auf
Deck 9 ist rund um die Uhr geöffnet.

Some of the Lido Buffet restaurants on
deck 9 are open 24 hours.

Da sich das zweistöckige Restaurant am Heck befindet, erlauben große Panoramafenster während des Essens einen spekta-
kulären Blick auf das Meer. Blickfang ist ein drei Meter hohes
Art déco-Wandbild mit Metallelementen gegenüber der Treppe und direkt hinter dem Kapitänstisch in einen Alkoven eingebettet. Ins Auge fällt auch sofort der hohe Kronleuchter im
Eingangsbereich, weitere kleinere Kronleuchter aus Swarovski-
Kristallglas finden sich im hinteren Teil des Restaurants. Die
geschwungene Doppeltreppe führt auf die obere Ebene, die
von Art déco-Säulen und -Bögen gestützt wird. Geschwungene
Glasbalkone geben den Blick auf die untere Ebene frei und
schaffen das Gefühl von räumlicher Weite.

BRITANNIA CLUB RESTAURANT

Dieses Restaurant wurde ganz neu auf einem Cunard Liner
geschaffen, denn auf der *Queen Mary 2,* wo das Konzept zum
ersten Mal eingeführt wurde, wurde eine Sektion des Britannia
Restaurant abgeteilt. In dem separaten, 190 m² großen Saal
können bis zu 84 Club-Gäste zwischen 18.30 und 21.00 Uhr
zu einem Zeitpunkt ihrer Wahl speisen. Auch dieser exklusive

with metallic elements, situated opposite of the stairs and
embedded in an alcove directly behind the captain's table, is
an eye catcher together with the large chandelier in the
entrance hall. Other smaller chandeliers made of Swarovski
crystal glass are situated in the aft part of the restaurant. The
sweeping staircase leads to the upper level, which is support-
ed by Art déco columns and arcs. The curved glass balconies
allow a view to the lower level and create a feeling of space.

BRITANNIA CLUB RESTAURANT

This restaurant is a complete novelty on a Cunard liner.
Already on *Queen Mary 2,* where the concept was introduced
for the first time, a section of the Britannia restaurant was
separated. Here the Brittania Club restaurant is a separate
room of 190 spm for up to 84 AA category guests that can
dine from 6.30 to 9 p. m. or at a time of their choosing.
The exclusive diningroom features a rich choice of Art déco
elements and a decorative ceiling with back-lit glass panels
and big round lights. On the inner side there are three sand-
blast glass walls with decorations and a bar. The tables

Speisesaal ist reich an Art déco-Elementen und verfügt über eine dekorative Decke mit hinterleuchteten Glasflächen und großen Rundleuchten. Auf der Innenseite befinden sich drei sandgestrahlte Glaswände mit Ornamenten und einer Bar, von den Tischen auf der gegenüberliegenden Seite schaut man aus großen Panoramafenstern auf das Meer.

DIE LIDO BÜFETT RESTAURANTS

Auf Deck 9 liegt das 24 Stunden geöffnete Büfettrestaurant Lido mit 468 Plätzen. Hier reicht von morgens bis abends zu allen Mahlzeiten, im Gegensatz zu den der Kabinenkategorie zugeordneten Restaurants, legere Kleidung aus. Morgens und mittags ist in dem 1100 m² großen Saal, der aus vier Büfettrestaurants besteht, freie Sitzplatzwahl. Dies ändert sich abends, wenn aus einem Teil des Lido ein Spezialitätenrestaurant wird, bei der eine von drei regionalen Küchen im Mittelpunkt steht und Service am Tisch geboten wird. Alle drei Tage wird gewechselt, so können Gäste im südamerikanischen Grill Asado speisen, die mexikanischen Spezialitäten des Aztec probieren oder im Jasmine traditionell asiatisch essen. Die Speisekarten orientieren sich an den besten Rezepten dieser Regionen und bieten viele landestypische Spezialitäten. Nach traditioneller südamerikanischer Art wird im Asado das Fleisch auf dem Grill gegart. Die Gäste können aus einer Auswahl von Gerichten aus der Rotisserie wählen, wie zum Beispiel geröstetem Chimichurri-Hähnchen oder argentinischen Lammkoteletts

on the opposite side allow a view of the sea through the large panoramic windows.

THE LIDO BUFFET RESTAURANTS

The Lido buffet restaurant with 468 seats, open 24 hours a day, is located on deck 9. Unlike the other restaurants associated with a specific cabin category, meals can be consumed here in casual dress from morning till night. In the morning and at lunchtime, the 1,100 sqm hall, with four buffet restaurants, offers open seating. This changes in the evening, when a part of the Lido becomes a speciality restaurant, highlighting one of three regional cuisines and offering waiter table service. Every three days, the menu changes. So guests can dine at the South American Grill Asado, try out the Mexican specialities at the Aztec or indulge in traditional Asian cuisine at the Jasmine. The menu focusses on the best recipes from these regions and offers many typical specialities. In the Asado, the meat is prepared on a grill in traditional South American style. The guests can choose from a variety of meals from the rotisserie, such as Roasted Chimmichuri Chicken or Argentinian Lamb Chops with Pistachio. The Aztec offers authentic Mexican cuisine. The guests can enjoy delicious meals such as Chile Relleno de Espinaca and Snapper Veracruzana in banana leaves. The Jasmine offers Pan-Asian cuisine with influences from Japan, Singapore, Indonesia, Thailand and China. Tantalizing dishes are inspired by many spices and unique cooking methods characteristic of the relevant region. The menu ranges from crispy duck to Char Siew Pau. The speciality restaurants are available for all guests at a surcharge of $ 10 per person, an advance table booking at the maître is recommended. All guests, who prefer casual dining, may visit the buffet stations in the Lido as formal attire is requested in the speciality restaurant.

THE GRILL RESTAURANTS: TOP CUISINE IN PRIVATE ATMOSPHERE

The Queens Grill and the Princess Grill restaurants follow a similar pattern of the award-winning Five Star Grills on board *Queen Mary 2* and *Queen Victoria*. The restaurants, both 254 sqm in size, which are reserved for guests of the

Im Courtyard können Suitengäste unter
freiem Himmel speisen.

The Courtyard offers al fresco dining for
the guests staying in the suites.

mit Pistazien. Im Aztec gibt es authentische mexikanische Küche. Gäste können sich auf leckere Gerichte wie Chile Rellenos
de Espinaca und Snapper Veracruzana im Bananenblatt freu-
en. Pan-asiatische Küche mit Einflüssen aus Japan, Singapur,
Indonesien, Thailand und China bietet das Jasmine. Die ver-
lockenden Speisen werden durch die vielen Gewürze und Gar-
methoden der jeweiligen Region bestimmt. Die Karte reicht
von knuspriger Ente bis zu Char Siew Pau. Die Spezialitäten-
restaurants stehen allen Gästen für einen Aufpreis von $ 10
pro Person zur Verfügung, eine Reservierung beim Maître wird
empfohlen. Neben dem Spezialitätenrestaurant stehen allen
Gästen, die auch an formellen Abenden gern leger speisen
möchten, die Büfett-Stationen im Lido zur Verfügung.

DIE GRILL-RESTAURANTS: SPITZEN-
KÜCHE IN PRIVATER ATMOSPHÄRE

Das Queens Grill und das Princess Grill Restaurant
folgen den Vorbildern der preisgekrönten Fünf-Sterne-
Grills der *Queen Mary 2* und der *Queen Victoria*. Die jeweils
254 m² großen Restaurants, die den Gästen der jeweiligen Suiten-Kategorien vorbehalten sind, befinden sich auf
Deck 11 und liegen einander gegenüber. Von der Außen- und
Innengestaltung her architektonisch gleich, sind beide Räume
in deutlich verschiedenen Art déco-Varianten dekoriert worden, um eine individuelle Atmosphäre in jedem Speisesaal zu
schaffen. Die Restaurants sind nach außen hin von anmutig
und sanft geschwungenen Panorama-Glas-Wänden abge-
schlossen und ragen über das darunter liegende Deck 10 he-
raus. Im Princess Grill stehen 122 Sitzplätze zur Verfügung, im
Queens Grill können bis zu 126 Passagiere speisen. In beiden
Restaurants werden À-la-carte-Menüs mit einer Kombination
klassischer Gerichte der Cunard-Küche und neue Kreationen
geboten. Gäste der Grill Suiten können zudem ihren eigenen
privaten Bar- und Loungebereich nutzen, der gleich neben
den Grill-Restaurants liegt und über einen Concierge-Service
verfügt. Hier werden der Nachmittagstee, Snacks und Cocktails serviert. Durch Türen im französischen Stil gelangen die
Gäste der Grills in den sogenannten Courtyard, einen exklusiven Innenhof, wo sie unter freiem Himmel essen können. Der
lauschige Innenhof mit Springbrunnen, Grünpflanzen und
Laternen als Hintergrundbeleuchtung bietet 40 Gästen Platz,
an klaren Abenden hat dieses Restaurant tausend Sterne.

respective suite categories, are situated on deck 11 opposite
of each other. The exterior and interior architecture is almost
identical, but both rooms differ distinctly in their Art
déco style, so as to create an individual dining atmosphere
in each dining room. The restaurants are enclosed by
elegantly and gently curved panoramic glass walls. Their
areas cantilever out over the side of the vessel above
deck 10. The Princess Grill has a capacity of 122 seats, and
up to 126 passengers can dine in the Queens Grill. Both
restaurants offer à la carte menus, an interesting combination of classic dishes of traditional Cunard cuisine and new
creations. The guests of the Grill suites can additionally use
their own private bar and lounge areas, located right next
to the Grill restaurants, complete with resident a Concierge.
The afternoon tea, snacks and cocktails are served here.
The guests of the Grill pass through French-style doors,

Die Wandkarte in der Midships Bar zeigt den Atlantischen Ozean (rechte Seite oben).

The chart on the wall in the Midships Bar depicts the Atlantic Ocean (right page, top).

Der Golden Lion Pub ist eine Institution und ein beliebter Treffpunkt auf Cunard-Schiffen (rechte Seite unten).

The Golden Lion Pub is a British institution and a popular meeting point on board Cunard ships. (right page, bottom)

BARS & CAFÉS

Die *Queen Elizabeth* bietet eine breite Auswahl an Bars, Cafés und Clubs für jeden Geschmack und jede Stimmung. Dabei wurde zum Teil auf bewährte Einrichtungen der *Queen Mary 2* und der *Queen Victoria* wie den Golden Lion Pub, den Commodore's Club, die Churchills Zigarrenlounge oder das Café Carinthia zurückgegriffen. Es gibt aber gegenüber den anderen beiden Flottenmitgliedern auch viel Neues: So wurde der von der *Queen Victoria* bekannte Wintergarten zu einer großzügig verglasten Garden Lounge umgestaltet und als Hommage an die *Queen Elizabeth 2* wurden der Yacht Club als Nachtclub und Diskothek sowie die zentrale Midships Bar in Erinnerung an die erste *Queen Elizabeth* wieder aufgenommen. Mit der Lido Pool Bar, der Pavillon Bar und der Empire Casino Bar können die Passagiere insgesamt zehn verschiedene Bars und Lounges besuchen.

CAFÉ CARINTHIA

Aufgrund der Popularität des gleichnamigen Cafés auf der *Queen Victoria* bietet diese einladende Lounge auch an Bord der *Queen Elizabeth* Platz für Gespräche und gesellige Runden. Durch seine zentrale Lage auf Deck 2 mit Blick auf die Grand Lobby ist das Café ein idealer Ort zum Sehen und Gesehen werden. Mit 92 Plätzen deutlich größer als auf der *Queen Victoria* (59 Sitze), ist das Café bis in den späten Abend geöffnet und bietet den ganzen Tag eine reichhaltige Auswahl an Kaffee- und Teesorten sowie frisch gebackene Croissants, Muffins, Sandwiches, Quiches und andere Snacks. Ein Highlight sind die Torten und Kuchen, die am Nachmittag angeboten werden. Das Café Carinthia ist wie eine alte französische Pâtisserie gestaltet, trotz der quirligen Umgebung machen es die bleiverglaste Decke, Marmor, die urige Theke und bequeme Sessel und Sofas zu einem gemütlichen Refugium.

GOLDEN LION PUB

Auf einen britischen Liner gehört auch ein traditioneller Pub, darum ist bei Cunard Line der Golden Lion Pub auch ein Klassiker. Der Pub liegt auf Deck 2 an der Plaza der Ladengalerie

before they enter the »Courtyard«, an exclusive patio area, where they can dine al fresco. The cosy patio with fountains, plants and lanterns as lighting has room for 40 guests. On clear evenings, this restaurant is illuminated by thousand of stars in the sky.

BARS & CAFÉS

Queen Elizabeth offers a great variety of bars, cafés and clubs to suit for every taste and every occasion. Only some of the proven facilities of *Queen Mary 2* and *Queen Victoria* such as the Golden Lion Pub, the Commodore's Club, Churchill's Cigar Lounge or Café Carinthia were installed here. In relation to the other two ships of the fleet *Queen Elizabeth* has indeed a lot of new things on offer. The well-known conservatory from *Queen Victoria* was redesigned, inspired by the glass houses at Kew Gardens and named Garden Lounge. The Yacht Club, paying homage to *Queen Elizabeth 2*, became a night club and discotheque, and the centrally located Midships Bar was revived in fond remembrance of the first *Queen Elizabeth*. Including the Lido pool bar, the Pavilion bar and the Empire Casino bar, the passengers can visit a total of ten different bars and lounges.

CAFÉ CARINTHIA

Due to the popularity of an identically named café on *Queen Victoria*, this inviting lounge offers space for conversations and for getting together on board *Queen Elizabeth*. Due to its central location on deck 2, overlooking the Grand Lobby, the café is an ideal place to see and be seen. It has 92 seats in comparison to *Queen Victoria* (59 seats). The café is open till late and offers a wide selection of coffees and teas as well as freshly baked croissants, muffins, sandwiches, quiches and other snacks throughout the whole day. Special highlights are gateaux and cakes that are offered in the afternoon. Café Carinthia is styled like an old French patisserie, and its ceiling with lead glazing, the marble, the rustic bar as well as comfortable armchairs and sofas make this place a cosy hideaway despite the lively ambience.

Die riesige, gewölbte Glaskuppel der Garden Lounge wurde den Londoner Kew Gardens nachempfunden.

The huge glass dome in the Garden Lounge was designed based on the greenhouses of Kew Gardens, London.

gegenüber dem Casino und ähnelt mehr noch als die gleichnamige Kneipe auf der *Queen Mary 2* einem traditionellen britischen Public House. Dies liegt zum einen an der Decke mit Messingfliesen zwischen mächtigen Balken, zum anderen an den Bleiglasfenstern und der Inneneinrichtung mit viel dunklem Holz, polierten Messingstangen an der Bar und schweren grünen Lederstühlen, -sesseln und -sofas. An die traditionelle Tafel, auf die mit Kreide die Tagesgerichte und Getränkepreise geschrieben werden, hat man ebenso gedacht wie an den Kamin, der allerdings mit Gas betrieben wird. Mittags gibt es hier traditionelles englisches Pub-Essen, von Fish 'n' Chips bis zu Shepherd's Pie bekommen die Gäste den authentischen Geschmack des Vereinigten Königreichs serviert, wo immer auf der Welt das Schiff sich gerade befindet. Auf allen 116 Sitzplätzen hat man gute Sicht auf moderne Plasmafernseher, auf denen Sportereignisse übertragen werden, und eine Vielzahl von Biersorten rundet das Erlebnis ab.

MIDSHIPS BAR

Diese Bar war ein zentraler Treffpunkt der Abendunterhaltung sowohl auf der ersten *Queen Elizabeth* als auch auf der *QE 2*,

GOLDEN LION PUB

On board a British liner a traditional pub is mandatory, and the Cunard Line's Golden Lion Pub is a classic for obvious reasons. The pub is located on deck 2, close to the plaza of the shopping mall opposite of the Casino and resembles much more than the identically named pub on *Queen Mary 2* a traditional British Public House. On one side this depends on the ceiling with brass tiles between mighty beams, on the other hand on the stained glass windows and the interior with a lot of dark wood, polished brass rods at the bar and heavy green leather chairs, armchairs and sofas. The prices of the daily meals and drinks are written with chalk on a traditional blackboard. There is even a fireplace, which however is fired by gas. At lunchtime, the guests can enjoy traditional English pub food ranging from Fish and Chips to Shepherd's Pie. The authentic taste of the British Isles is guaranteed, regardless of the actual position of the ship. All 116 seats are arranged in such a way that the guests can watch sport programmes on modern plasma TVs. A wide selection of international beers contribute to the overall pub experience.

dort wurde sie nach einem Umbau 1994 zur Chart Room Bar. Mittschiffs gelegen – der Name suggeriert es bereits – kann man von hier auf der Steuerbordseite von Deck 3 die gesamte Lobby überblicken. Glasvitrinen an den Wänden enthalten Erinnerungsstücke von der ersten *Queen Elizabeth,* wie Bordtelefone aus Bakelit oder originale Reisetickets. Ein Modell des Liners gehört zu den besonderen Attraktionen. Gleich daneben beherrscht ein großes Wandbild den Hintergrund. Es zeigt eine Karte der Atlantikstrecke und ist nach dem Vorbild aus dem Speisesaal der Ersten Klasse auf der *Queen Mary* gefertigt. 48 Sitzplätze stehen hier auf 130 m² zur Verfügung, ein Klavierspieler sorgt abends für Unterhaltung.

GARDEN LOUNGE

Vorbild für dieses optische Highlight auf Deck 9 waren die Gewächshäuser der Londoner Kew Gardens. Die 490 m² große,

MIDSHIPS BAR

This bar was a central meeting point before the evening entertainment on the first *Queen Elizabeth* as well as on *QE 2,* where after a refit in 1994, the bar was named Chart Room bar. As its name implies, the bar is located mid-ships, from here on the starboard side of deck 3 one can overlook the entire lobby. The glass cabinets in the walls feature memorabilia from the first *Queen Elizabeth* such as telephones made of Bakelite or historic tickets. A model ship of the liner is one of the special attractions. Right next to it, in the background a large painting dominates the wall. It shows a chart of the Atlantic route and was designed and built based on the one in the First Class dininghall an board *Queen Mary.* This bar offers 48 seats covering an area of 130 sqm. The guest can enjoy the evening listening to live piano music.

lichtdurchflutete Garden Lounge ist ein Wintergarten mit ge-
wölbtem Glasdach und freiem Blick in den Himmel, in dem
es sich hervorragend in luftiger Atmosphäre sitzen lässt. Dazu
tragen auch die Wandbilder von Garten-Partys bei, die durch
ihre Maltechnik den Raum noch weiter und offener erscheinen lassen. Die Garden Lounge ist nach einem Veranstaltungs-
raum auf der ersten *Queen Elizabeth* benannt und verfügt über
70 Plätze. Das Interieur ist ganz im Kolonialstil gehalten, es
dominieren Rattan- und Korbmöbel, viele Grünpflanzen sowie
Palmen. Auch hier wird der traditionelle Nachmittagstee mit
Sandwiches, Scones mit Clotted Cream und diversen Kuchen-
und Törtchenleckereien zelebriert, an der Saftbar werden Mix-
turen und reine Säfte aus exotischen Früchten angeboten. An
ausgewählten Seetagen wird hier für einen Aufpreis von $ 25
pro Person eine Champagner Tea Time angeboten. Gelegent-
liche »Supper Clubs« am Abend bieten die Möglichkeit, das
Dinner mit Tanz unter den Sternen zu kombinieren. Zu Live-

GARDEN LOUNGE

The glasshouses at Kew Gardens in London inspired this
highlight on deck 9. The 490 sqm, light-flooded Garden
Lounge is a conservatory with a magnificent vaulted glass
ceiling allowing vision of the sky. The place is airy and it is easy
to relax here. Murals of garden parties make the room look
even more spacious and wider. The Garden Lounge is named
after a room on the first *Queen Elizabeth* and offers 70 seats.
The interior totally in the colonial style, with rattan and wicker
furniture, many foliage plants and palm trees. Here, the
traditional afternoon tea can be enjoyed eating sandwiches,
scones with clotted cream and a large variety of delicious
cakes and pastries. The juice bar offers mixed and pure
juices made from exotic fruits. On select days at sea, a champagne afternoon tea service offered at a surcharge of $ 25
per person. Occasional »Supper Clubs« in the evening are a

Musik werden dabei Fingerfood und andere kleine Gaumen-freuden serviert.

YACHT CLUB

Das gläserne Dreiviertelrund des Yacht Clubs mit seinen mannshohen Fenstern, die einen 270 Grad weiten Rundblick über das Deck und die See bieten, fällt auf Deck 10 sofort ins Auge. Auf der *Queen Victoria* »Hemispheres« genannt, ist dieser Veranstaltungs- und Nachtclub nur äußerlich baugleich. Der Yacht Club soll das geschätzte Ambiente des beliebten Vorgängers am Achterdeck der *Queen Elizabeth 2* würdig fortführen. So steht gleich am Eingang des in seiner Einrichtung nautisch beeinflussten Raums ein Modell der *QE 2* aus reinem Silber. 1800 Stunden benötigten die Silberschmiede des berühmten britischen Juweliers Asprey, bis sie dieses Meisterwerk ihrer Kunst mit der Hand gefertigt hatten. In den Fries der Umrandung des Glasdachs sind maritime Signalflaggen eingearbeitet, die Tanzfläche ziert ein riesiger Kompass aus Holzintarsien. Das mit einem Kronleuchter und einer Bar geschmückte 220 m² große Rund bietet Sitzplätze für 97 Gäste und wird tagsüber für Vorträge, Seminare und Kurse genutzt. Abends verwandelt sich der Yacht Club in einen mondänen Nachtclub mit Musik, der bis in die frühen Morgenstunden geöffnet ist.

CHURCHILLS ZIGARRENLOUNGE

Beim Eintreten in die mit schweren Glastüren abgeschlossene Zigarrenlounge steht man vor einem großen Wandbild mit einem Foto des Namensgebers. In schweren Ledersesseln finden elf Gäste Platz, neben exquisiter Rauchware in reichhaltiger Auswahl werden hier Spezialitäten wie Jahrgangsflaschen Armagnac, Cognac, Portwein, Madeira und schottischer Whisky angeboten. Die holzgetäfelte Lounge bietet die einzige Gelegenheit, in öffentlichen Räumen zu rauchen.

COMMODORE CLUB

Der Commodore's Club wurde als Erfolgsmodell von der *Queen Mary 2* und der *Queen Victoria* übernommen. Der Club ist als Aussichtslounge konzipiert und liegt am Bug auf Deck 10.

good option to combine dining with dancing under a star-lit sky. Finger food and other culinary delicacies are served accompanied by live music.

YACHT CLUB

The eye-catching glass thee-quarter circle of the Yacht Club with its tall windows offers 270 degrees of panoramic view over the deck towards the sea. Only on the face of it the construction resembles »Hemispheres«, the venue and night club on *Queen Victoria*. Yacht Club will strive with dignity to maintain the esteemed ambience of its popular predecessor on the aft deck of *Queen Elizabeth 2*. Right next to the entrance of the room in nautical style, is a model ship of *QE 2*, hand-made in pure silver. The silversmiths of the famous British jewellers Asprey needed 1,800 hours to produce it. Maritime signal flags were inserted in the frame around the glass roof and the wooden dance floor is compass-shaped. The 220 sqm rotunda, decorated with a chandelier and a bar, offers seats for 97 guests. During daytime it is used for lectures, seminars and courses. In the evening, the Yacht Club turns into a chic night club with music performances. It is open until the early hours of the morning.

CHURCHILL'S CIGAR LOUNGE

After entering the Cigar Lounge through the heavy glass doors, passengers find themselves in front of a large wall painting featuring a photograph of the Churchil. The heavy leather armchairs can accommodate eleven guests, that are able to enjoy a large assortment of exquisite tobacco products as well as specialities such as vintage Armagnac, cognac, Port wine, Madeira wine and Scotch whisky. The wood-panelled lounge offers the only chance of smoking in a public area.

COMMODORE CLUB

The Commodore Club was based on the successful rooms on *Queen Mary 2* and *Queen Victoria*. The Club was designed as an observation lounge, located on deck 10 at the bow. From

Von hier aus genießt man den gleichen Blick über die weite See wie die Offiziere auf der Brücke. Zumindest bis zum Einbruch der Dämmerung, denn nachts wird die hohe Fensterfront mit Stoffjalousien verdunkelt, damit die Wachhabenden auf der Brücke nicht durch das Licht geblendet werden. Für den besseren Weitblick ist sogar ein Teleskop aufgestellt worden, mit dem man detailliert die Wellen oder den Horizont betrachten kann. Durch den atemberaubenden Ausblick über den Schiffsbug und viele gemütliche Sitzecken ist der Club der perfekte Ort, um tagsüber abzuschalten, einen Roman zu lesen oder einfach nur die Welt an sich vorbeiziehen zu lassen.

Durch gut gepolsterte Ledersofas, Sessel mit hohen Armlehnen, Tische für Kartenspiele, Beistelltischchen mit Leselampen und die Verwendung von viel Messing und Mahagoni bei Geländern, die als Raumteiler dienen, kommt das Am-

here, visitors enjoy an identical view out to the open sea as the officers on the bridge. The tall window fronts are darkened with blinds at night time, so that the watch-keeper on the bridge is not blinded by light. There is even a telescope for more detailed news the waves horizon in the distance. Due to the breathtaking view across the ship's bow and many cosy lounge areas, the Club is the perfect place to relax all day long, reading novels or just letting the world pass by.

The richly upholstered leather sofas, the armchairs with high arm rests, the card tables, side tables with reading lamps and the lavish usage of brass and mahogany for the handrails, that serve as partitions, creates the ambience of an old-established London Club. However women are admitted here. The entrances to the 400 sqm lounge with

Am Eingang zum Commodore's
Club hängen Ölgemälde der neuen
Cunard-Liner in Bullaugen-Optik von
Marinemaler Robert G. Lloyd.

At the entrance of the Commodores Club
porthole-shaped paintings of the new
Cunard liner are on display, created by
the marine painter Robert G. Lloyd.

biente eines altehrwürdigen Londoner Clubs auf, wobei, im Gegensatz zu diesen, Frauen auf dem Schiff selbstverständlich Zutritt haben. An den Eingängen der 400 m² großen Lounge mit 170 Plätzen stehen Glasvitrinen mit detailgetreuen Modellen der aktuellen Queens-Flotte. An Backbord ein ca. 1,50 Meter langes Modell der *Queen Victoria* von Maritime Replica im Maßstab 1:163, an Steuerbord die ebenso lange *Queen Mary 2,* natürlich im kleineren Maßstab von 1:192. Mittschiffs über der Bar ist ein Modell der *Queen Elizabeth* aufgestellt, das mit etwa 50 Zentimetern deutlich kleiner ist als die Repliken an den Eingängen. Dort hängen auch jeweils drei Wandbilder von Robert G. Lloyd, die in Bullaugenoptik alle drei neuen Queens sowie den historischen Augenblick darstellen, als *Queen Elizabeth 2, Queen Mary 2* und *Queen Victoria* sich in Southampton trafen.

170 seats feature glass cabinets with detailed miniature model ships of the present Queens' fleet: on port side is housed an approximately 1.50 metre long model of *Queen Victoria,* made by Maritime Replica in the scale of 1:163, is displayed while on starboard side there is a model of *Queen Mary 2* of equal length, in the scale of 1:192. Midships above the bar, one can find a model of *Queen Elizabeth* which is around 50 centimetres and definitely smaller than the replicas found at the entrances. There are also three wall paintings in bull's eye perspective by Robert G. Lloyd, showing the three new Queens as well as memorating that precious historical moment, when *Queen Elizabeth 2, Queen Mary 2* and *Queen Victoria* had a Rendezvous is Southampton.

GENTLEMEN BITTEN ZUM TANZ
GENTLEMEN ASK TO A DANCE

Anfang der 1970er-Jahre stellte die Reederei fest, dass der Anteil der alleinreisenden Frauen in fortgeschrittenem Alter auf Kreuzfahrten stark gestiegen war. Fast alle dieser Damen gingen allein auf Kreuzfahrt, weil sie verwitwet waren, ergaben vorsichtige Nachforschungen. Vor allem die beiden Weltkriege hatten ihren Tribut gefordert, und Schiffsreisen schienen bei den Witwen besonders beliebt zu sein. Cunard reagierte und besann sich darauf, dass bereits in den Goldenen Zwanzigern die sogenannten Eintänzer sehr beliebt waren und bei den Damen sehr gut ankamen. Damals waren es vor allem aus der Armee entlassene Offiziere, die sich auf diese Art und Weise ihren Lebensunterhalt verdienen mussten. Da sie sich ausgezeichnet zu benehmen wussten und elegante Kleidung tragen konnten, waren sie bei Lokalbetreibern wie bei alleinstehenden Frauen geschätzt.

1972 führte Cunard auf der *Queen Elizabeth 2* erstmals das Konzept des Gentleman Hosts ein, vier charmante Herren waren für die Unterhaltung der alleinstehenden Damen engagiert worden. Heute fahren regelmäßig bis zu sechs von ihnen auf *Queen Elizabeth* und *Queen Victoria*, bis zu zehn Gentleman Hosts sind es gar auf der *Queen Mary 2*. Das erfolgreiche Konzept wurde inzwischen von vielen Reedereien übernommen. Das Alter eines Gentleman Hosts liegt der Zielgruppe angemessen zwischen 45 und 70 Jahren. Sie müssen alleinstehend sein, über geschliffene Umgangsformen verfügen und ausnahmslos einen seriösen persönlichen sowie beruflichen Hintergrund haben. Rauchen ist ebenso unerwünscht wie regelmäßiges Trinken von Alkohol. Wichtigste Voraussetzung ist jedoch, alle Tänze perfekt zu beherrschen. In der Regel sind die Gentleman Hosts Rentner oder finanziell unabhängig, fast immer sind es Amerikaner oder Engländer, meistens Rechtsanwälte, Lehrer, Piloten oder Unternehmer im Ruhestand. Gentleman Hosts sind eine Art männliche Hostessen, das weibliche Pendant gibt es bei Cunard Line nicht, weil die Zahl alleinreisender Männer verschwindend gering ist.

Die infrage kommenden Herren werden von einer Agentur aus Chicago handverlesen. Die Kandidaten müssen einen Eignungstest bestehen und sich auf ihre Manieren und Fähigkeiten zum Small Talk prüfen lassen. Auch die Tanzschritte werden dort unter die Lupe genommen. Standardschritte,

auch in lateinamerikanischen Tänzen, reichen aus, in altersgemäßem Tempo und ohne akrobatische Verrenkungen, aber Rhythmusgefühl muss vorhanden sein. Außerdem bekommen die angehenden Gentleman Hosts Schulungen und Tipps, wie sie sich elegant aus schwieriger Situation lösen können, ohne die Gesprächs- oder Tanzpartnerin vor den Kopf zu stoßen. Als Entlohnung erhalten die distinguierten Herren die Kreuzfahrt, An- und Abreise sowie Essen und bestimmte Getränke zu den Mahlzeiten kostenlos. Sie haben ein gewisses Budget an den Bars, um die Damen auch mal einladen zu können und bekommen Rabatt für Reinigungs- und Kommunikationskosten. Dabei gehören die Gentleman Hosts nicht zur Crew, sie wohnen in Innenkabinen auf einem der unteren Decks und essen im Passagierrestaurant.

Die Aufgabe der beim Casting erfolgreichen Herren auf den Schiffen geht über das Tanzen hinaus. Die Gentleman Hosts, die am ersten Tag der Reise auf einer Single Party vom Kreuzfahrtdirektor vorgestellt werden, sollen den alleinreisenden Damen Gesellschaft leisten, die Reise angenehm gestalten und keine Einsamkeit aufkommen lassen. Die Kavaliere alter Schule sind meist auch glänzende Unterhalter, in der Lage, unverkrampfte Gespräche zu führen, Kontakte zwischen wildfremden Menschen zu vermitteln und eine Atmosphäre zu schaffen, in der sich alle Beteiligten wohlfühlen. Darüber hinaus sind sie immer im Dienst, wenn an Bord irgendwo Orchestermusik spielt, von der Unterrichtsstunde mit Tanzlehrer am Vormittag bis zum Ende der Bälle im Queen's Room kurz nach Mitternacht. Immer mit dem Blick für Passagierinnen, die bei diesen Veranstaltungen allein in ihrem Sessel sitzen oder keinen Tanzpartner finden. Doch die Gentlemen sind keine Gigolos, sie müssen vertraglich festgelegte Regeln befolgen. Glücksspiele im bordeigenen Casino und intime Beziehungen zu Gästen führen zu einer fristlosen Kündigung, die sofortige Heimreise ist dann auf eigene Kosten anzutreten. Gegenseitige Kabinenbesuche mit alleinreisenden Damen sind ebenfalls untersagt, wer erwischt wird, muss das Schiff verlassen. Gegen echte Gefühle helfen aber auch keine Verträge. So ist es auch schon vorgekommen, dass sich ein Gentleman Host und eine Passagierin so ineinander verliebten, dass der Mann sofort seinen Dienst quittierte. Für immer, denn kurze Zeit später läuteten die Hochzeitsglocken.

At the beginning of the 1970s, the shipping company had realised that a considerably increased quota of single women of higher age travelled on cruises. The initial researches showed that the reason for these women travelling alone was their marital status: they were widows. Specially the two World Wars had taken their toll, but sea voyages were very much in vogue with the widows. Cunard reacted quickly and remembered the fact that during the Golden Twenties, »male taxi dancers« had been very popular and had made a good impression on the ladies. At that time, the dancers were all retired military officers, who had to make a living with this job. Because they were educated excellent, had good manners and dressed well, their servies were highly appreciated by the owners of dancing halls as well as single women.

For the first time in 1972, Cunard introduced the concept of the gentleman hosts on board of *Queen Elizabeth 2*. Four charming gentlemen were hired to entertain single ladies. Today, up to six of them are permanently on *Queen Elizabeth* and on *Queen Victoria,* and even up to ten gentleman hosts are available on *Queen Mary 2*. In the meantime, this successful concept was adopted by many other shipping companies. The age of a gentleman host ranges between 45 to 70 years, often matching the target group. They have to be single, possess excellent manners and without exception must have a serious personal and professional background. Smoking is definitely looked upon, as well the regular consumption of alcohol. However, the most important condition is to be a perfect dancer. Usually the gentleman hosts are retired or financially independent; the majority of them are Americans or English, often retired lawyers, teachers, pilots or businessmen. Gentleman hosts are a kind of male »hostesses«, the female equivalent does not exist on the Cunard Ships, as the number of single travelling men is negligibly small.

The appropriate gentlemen are hand-picked by a Chicago-based agency. The candidates have to pass a qualifying examination and are cross-checked for their manners and small talk abilities. The dancing steps are carefully examined too. Standard dance steps and also Latin American dances, are sufficient, with an age-adequate performance without contortions. However a rhythm feeling is a must. Furthermore, the gentleman hosts' candidates have to undergo and pass training sessions. They are given and imbibe several valuable advice as how to smoothly handle difficult situations without disappointing their conversation or dancing partners.

The gentlemen once chosen, travel free on board, and their travel costs to and from the ship are paid. All meals and certain beverages served with the meals are available free of charge as well. They have a certain budget in the bars, in order to be able to invite the ladies for a drink from time to time. Furthermore, they receive for a discount for the cleaning service and for comunication expenses. However, the gentleman hosts are not members of the crew, they are accommodated in inner cabins on one of the lower decks and dine in the passengers' restaurants.

The tasks of those gentlemen, who successfully passed the test, exceed dancing on the ships by far. The gentleman hosts are introduced by the cruise director on the first day of the voyage during a »Single Party«. They are asked to keep the single travelling ladies company and make their voyages as comfortable as possible and to avoid any loneliness on the ladies side. The educated gentlemen are mostly excellent entertainers. They are able to conduct relaxed conversations, arrange meetings for total strangers and create an atmosphere of well-being and friendliness for all on board. On top of that, they are always in service; e.g. when an orchestra plays music on board, during the dance lessons in the at morning, or shortly after midnight, when the balls in the Queen's Room have finished. They need to always keep a good eye on female passengers, who sit alone in their armchairs or do not find a dancing partner. However, the gentlemen are no gigolos and they must obey the stipulated rules. Gambling in the casinos and intimate relations with guests will result in an immediate dismissal, followed by a trip back home at their own expenses straightaway. Visiting single ladies in their cabins is also forbidden. If caught, a gentleman host has to leave the ship. However, stipulated rules cannot avoid the development of true emotional feelings. Once, a gentleman host fell in love with a female passenger; he quit his job immediately and forever. Wedding bells could be heard ringing soon afterwards.

DIE QUEENS IM ÜBERBLICK
A SYNOPSIS OF THE QUEENS

	Queen Elizabeth	Queen Elizabeth 2	Queen Elizabeth
Länge (über alles) Lenght (over all)	301 Meter 301 Meter	293,5 Meter 293,5 Meter	294 Meter 294 Meter
Breite Width	36 Meter 36 Meter	32 Meter 32 Meter	32,30 Meter 32,30 Meter
Höhe **(Kiel bis Mastspitze)** Height (Bottom Line to Mast Top)	71 Meter 71 Meter	62 Meter 62 Meter	64,60 Meter 64,60 Meter
Tonnage **(in jeweils gültiger Maßeinheit)** Tonnage	83 673 GT	65 863 BRT 70 327 BRZ (nach Umbau 1994) (after conversion in 1994)	90 900 BRZ
Tiefgang Max Summerdraft	13 Meter 13 Meter	9,9 Meter 9,9 Meter	8 Meter 8 Meter
Maximalgeschwindigkeit Full Sea Speed	32,5 Knoten 32,5 Knots	34,6 Knoten 34,6 Knots	24,3 Knoten 24,3 Knots
Betriebsgeschwindigkeit Manoeuver Speed	28,5 Knoten 28,5 Knots	28,5 Knoten 28,5 Knots	21,7 Knoten 21,7 Knots
PS HP	160 000 PS 160 000 HP	130 000 PS 130 000 HP	140 000 PS 140 000 HP
Passagiere Passengers	2283	1850	2068
Crew Crew	1100	900	1003
Werft Shipyard	John Brown, Clydebank Scotland	John Brown, Clydebank Scotland	Fincantieri Monfalcone, Italy

	Queen Elizabeth	Queen Elizabeth 2	Queen Elizabeth
Kiellegung Keel Laying	6.10.1932	5.7.1965	2.7.2009
Stapellauf/Ausdocken Launching	27.9.1938	20.9.1967	5.12.2010
Taufe Naming Ceremony	27.9.1938	20.9.1967	11.10.2010
Taufpatin Godmother	Queen Elizabeth (Gattin von König George VI.) (Wife of King George VI.)	Queen Elizabeth II.	Queen Elizabeth II.
Heimathafen Port of Registry	Liverpool	Southampton	Southampton
Flagge Flag	Großbritannien Great Britain	Großbritannien Great Britain	Großbritannien Great Britain
Raumzahl **(Tonnage geteilt durch** **Passagierzahl)** Tonnage divided by Passengers	36,65	38,01	43,21
Außerdienststellung Decommissioning	1972 in Hongkong nach einem Feuer gesunken und abgewrackt 1972, Hong Kong, sunk after fire and demolished	November 2008 geplant als Hotelschiff an The Palm Jumeirah, Dubai November 2008 scheduled to become a floating hotel at »The Palm Jumeirah«, Dubai	–

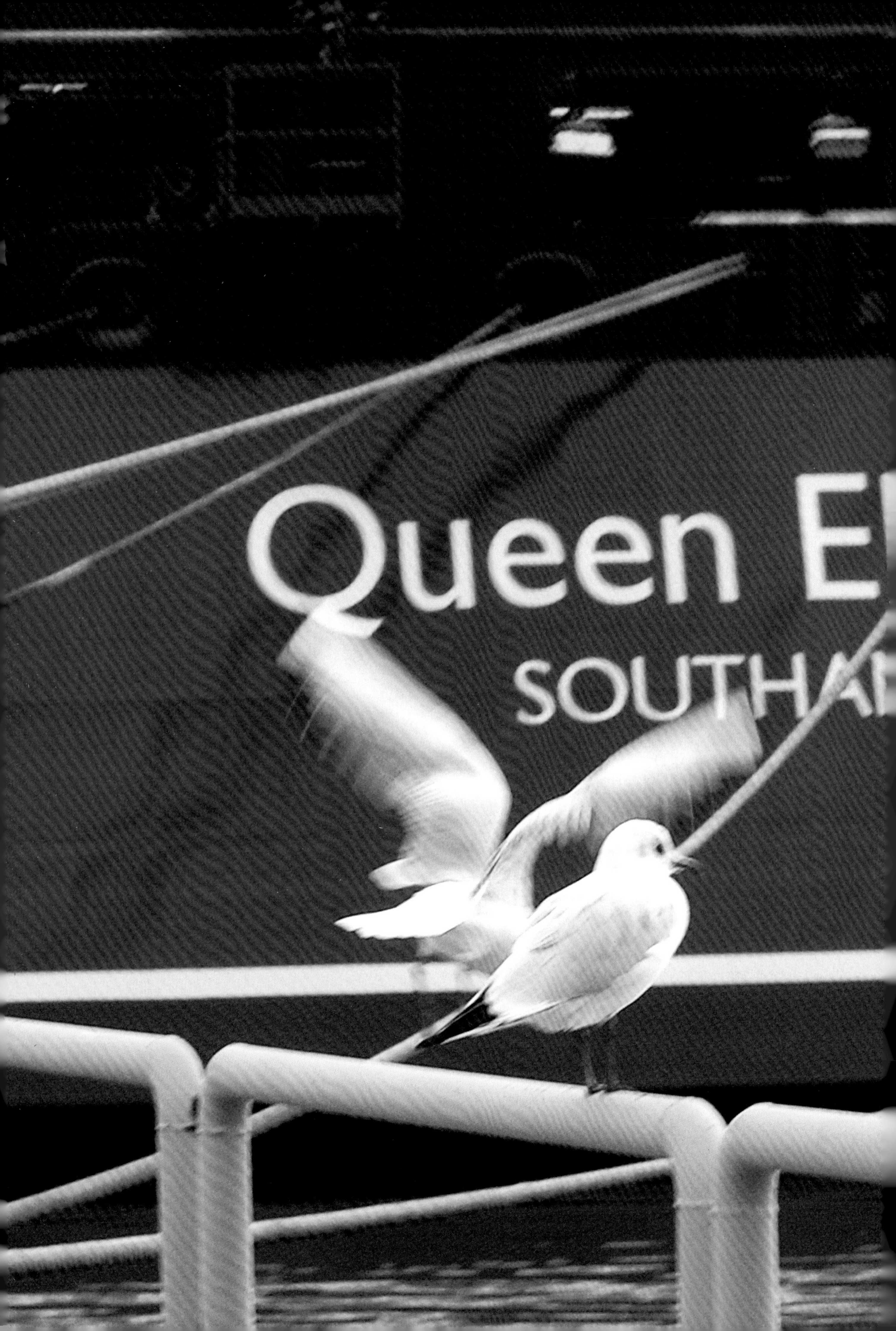
Queen El
SOUTHA